Plenty

David Hare is the author of thirty-two full-length plays for the stage, seventeen of which have been presented at the National Theatre. They include *Slag*, *The Great Exhibition*, *Brassneck* (with Howard Brenton), *Knuckle*, *Fanshen*, *Teeth 'n' Smiles*, *Plenty*, *A Map of the World*, *Pravda* (with Howard Brenton), *The Bay at Nice*, *The Secret Rapture*, *Racing Demon*, *Murmuring Judges*, *The Absence of War*, *Skylight*, *Amy's View*, *The Blue Room* (from Schnitzler), *The Judas Kiss*, *Via Dolorosa*, *My Zinc Bed*, *The Breath of Life*, *The Permanent Way*, *Stuff Happens*, *The Vertical Hour*, *Gethsemane*, *Berlin/Wall*, *The Power of Yes*, *South Downs* and *Behind the Beautiful Forevers*. His many screenplays for film and television include *Licking Hitler*, *Wetherby*, *Damage*, *The Hours*, *The Reader*, *Page Eight*, *Turks & Caicos* and *Salting the Battlefield*. He has also written English adaptations of plays by Brecht, Gorky, Chekhov, Pirandello, Ibsen and Lorca.

DAVID HARE

Plenty

ff

FABER & FABER

First published in 1978
by Faber and Faber Limited
The Bindery, 51 Hatton Garden
London EC1N 8HN

This edition reset with revisions, 2016

Typeset by Country Setting, Kingsdown, Kent CT14 8ES
Printed and bound in the UK by CPI Group (UK) Ltd, Croydon CR0 4YY

David Hare is hereby identified as the author
of this work in accordance with Section 77 of the
Copyright, Designs and Patents Act 1988

A CIP record for this book
is available from the British Library

ISBN 978-0-571-33613-5

Author's Note

Plenty was written in the late 1970s, alongside a
companion piece, *Licking Hitler*, which I wrote for BBC
Television at the same time. The TV play concentrated
on a woman's experience of the Second World War, and
only skipped quickly through her post-war years at the
end. *Plenty* took the opposite course, touching briefly on
my heroine's career behind the lines in occupied France,
and concentrating instead on her post-war life.

I was moved to write the play for two reasons. First, I felt
very strongly that women's experience was missing from
accounts of the official history of the period. But second,
I had read that the marriages of 75 per cent of the female
agents for the Special Operations Executives had ended
in divorce. It seemed that their work in the war had left
them either with memories or expectations which made
it very hard for them to settle back into civilian life.

Plenty was first presented in London in my own
production at the National Theatre in April 1978, with
Kate Nelligan playing Susan Traherne and Stephen
Moore as Brock. Its American premiere was at Arena
Stage in Washington DC in 1980 with Blair Brown
playing Susan and John Glover, Brock. Joe Papp
produced the play at the Public Theater in New York
in 1982, once more with Kate Nelligan as Susan, but
this time with Ed Herrmann as Brock. This production
transferred to the Plymouth Theatre on Broadway in 1983.

In 1985, the film of *Plenty* was released, directed by Fred
Schepisi, with Meryl Streep playing Susan, Charles Dance
as Brock, and with John Gielgud as Leonard Darwin.

The play was last seen in the West End of London at the Albery Theatre in 1999 with Cate Blanchett playing Susan and Julian Wadham as Brock.

David Hare
September 2016

Characters

Susan Traherne

Alice Park

Raymond Brock

Codename Lazar

A Frenchman

Sir Leonard Darwin

Mick

Louise

M. Aung

Mme Aung

Dorcas Frey

John Begley

Sir Andrew Charleson

Another Frenchman

Plenty was first performed at the Lyttelton Theatre, London, on 7 April 1978. The cast was as follows:

Susan Traherne Kate Nelligan
Alice Park Julie Covington
Raymond Brock Stephen Moore
Codename Lazar Paul Freeman
Frenchman Robert Ralph
Sir Leonard Darwin Basil Henson
Mick David Schofield
Louise Gil Brailey
M Aung Kristopher Kum
Mme Aung Me Me Lai
Dorcas Frey Lindsay Duncan
John Begley Tom Durham
Sir Andrew Charleson Frederick Treves
Another Frenchman Timothy Davies

Directed by David Hare
Settings by Hayden Griffin
Costumes by Deirdre Clancy
Music by Nick Bicât

Plenty was revived in the Newman Theatre of the Public Theatre, New York, on 4 October 2016. The cast was as follows:

Susan Traherne Rachel Weisz
Alice Park Emily Bergl
Raymond Brock Corey Stoll
Codename Lazar Ken Barnett
Frenchman Benjamin Thys
Sir Leonard Darwin Byron Jennings
Mick LeRoy McClain
Louise Dani de Waal
M Aung Pun Bandhu
Mme Aung Ann Sanders
Dorcas Liesel Allen Yeager
John Begley Tim Nicolai
Sir Andrew Charleson Paul Niebanck
Another Frenchman Mike Iveson

Directed by David Leveaux
Settings by Mike Britton
Lighting Designer David Weiner
Costumes by Jess Goldstein
Original Music and Sound Design David Van Tieghem

PLENTY

For Kate

Knightsbridge. Easter 1962.

A wooden floor. At the back of the stage high windows give the impression of a room which has been stripped bare. Around the floor are packing cases full of fine objects. At the front lies a single mattress, on which a naked man is sleeping face downwards.

Susan sits on one of the packing cases. In her middle thirties, she is thin and well presented. She wastes no energy. She now rolls an Old Holborn and lights it.

Alice comes in from the street, a blanket over her head. She carries a small tinfoil parcel. She is small-featured, slightly younger and busier than Susan. She wears jeans. She drops the blanket and shakes the rain off herself.

Alice I don't know why anybody lives in this country. No wonder everyone has colds all the time. Even what they call passion, it still comes at you down a blocked nose.

Susan smokes quietly. Alice is distracted by some stray object which she tosses into a packing case. The man stirs and turns over. He is middle-aged, running to fat and covered in dried blood. Susan cues Alice.

Susan And the food.

Alice Yeah. The wet. The cold. The flu. The food. The loveless English. How is he?

Susan Fine.

Alice kneels down beside him.

Alice The blood is spectacular.

Susan The blood is from his thumb.

Alice takes his penis between her thumb and forefinger.

Alice Turkey neck and turkey gristle, isn't that what they say?

A pause. Susan smokes.

Are you sure he's OK?

Susan He had a couple of Nembutal and twelve fingers of Scotch. It's nothing else, don't worry.

Alice And a fight.

Susan A short fight.

Alice takes the tinfoil parcel and opens it. Steam rises.

Alice Chinese takeaway. Want some?

Susan It's six o'clock in the morning.

Alice Sweet and sour prawn.

Susan No thanks.

Alice You should. You worked as hard as I did. When we started last night, I didn't think it could be done.

Alice gestures round the empty room. Then eats. Susan watches, then gets up and stands behind her with a key.

Susan It's a Yale. There's a mortise as well but I've lost the key. There's a cleaning lady next door, should you want one, her work's good but don't try talking about the blacks. You have a share in that garden in the centre of the square, you know all those trees and flowers they keep locked up in case some passer-by feels like enjoying himself. It's yours if you can stand the Knightsbridge conversation. Tribal code, tricky till you crack it. Koochie is how you address your dog. Gucci is a shop, that sort of thing. The milkman calls daily, again he's nice, but don't touch the yoghurt, it's green, we call it Venusian sperm. (*Pause.*) Good luck with your girls.

Susan turns to go. Alice gets up.

Alice Are you sure you can't stay? I think you'd like them.

Susan Unmarried mothers, I don't think I'd get on.

Alice I'm going to ring round at nine o'clock. If you just stayed on for a couple of hours . . .

Susan You don't really want that, nobody would.

Pause.

Alice What do I tell your husband?

Susan Tell him the truth.

Alice It's just it was his home when he went to sleep.

Susan I've given it to you.

Alice So I tell him you've left?

Susan Tell him I left with nothing that was his. I just walked out on him. Everything to go.

Susan smiles again and goes out. There is a pause. The man stirs again at the front of the stage. Alice stands still holding the sweet and sour prawn.

Brock Darling.

Brock is still asleep. His eyes don't open as he turns over. Alice watches very beadily. There is a long pause. Then he murmurs:

What's for breakfast?

Alice Fish.

SCENE TWO

St Benoît. November 1943.

Darkness. From the dark the sound of the wireless. From offstage a beam of light flashes irregularly, cutting up through the night. Then back to dark.

Announcer Ici Londres. Les voix de la liberté. Ensuite quelques messages personnels. Mon Oncle Albert a Perdu son Chien. Mon–Oncle–Albert–A–Perdu–Son–Chien.

A heavy thump in the darkness. Then the sound of someone running towards the noise. A small amount of light shows us the scene. Lazar is trying to disentangle himself from his parachute. He has landed at the edge of the wood. At the back Susan runs on from a great distance, wrapped in a greatcoat against the cold. She has a scarf round her face so that only her eyes can be seen. She is extremely nervous and vulnerable, and her uncertainty makes her rude and abrupt.

Susan Eh, qu'est-ce que vous faites ici?

Lazar Ah rien. Laisse-moi un moment, je peux tout expliquer.

Susan takes a revolver from her pocket and moves towards him. She stoops down, feels the edge of Lazar's parachute.

Susan Donnez-moi votre sac.

Lazar throws across the satchel which has been tied to his waist. Susan looks through it, then puts the gun back in her pocket.

And your French is not good.

Susan moves quickly away to listen for sounds in the night. Lazar watches, then speaks quietly to her back. Lazar is a codename; he is, of course, English.

Lazar Where am I?

Susan Please be quiet. I can't hear when you speak. (*Pause.*) There's a road. Through the wood. Gestapo patrol.

Lazar I see.

Susan I thought I heard something.

Lazar Are you waiting for supplies?

Susan On the hour. There's meant to be a drop. I thought it was early, that's why I flashed.

Lazar I'm sorry. We had to take advantage of your light. We were losing fuel. I'm afraid I'm meant to be eighty miles on. Can you . . . could you tell me where I am?

Susan You've landed near a village called St Benoît. It's close to a town called Poitiers, all right?

Lazar Yes. I think. I have heard of it, you know.

Pause. She half turns but still does not look at him.

Susan Hadn't you better take that thing off?

Lazar We are in the same racket, I suppose?

Susan Well, we're pretty well dished if we aren't. Did you spot any movement as you came down?

Lazar None at all. We just picked out your light.

Susan If you didn't see anything I'd like to hold on. We need the drop badly – explosives and guns.

Lazar Have you come out on your own?

A pause. He has taken off his jump-suit. Underneath he is dressed as a French peasant. Now he puts a beret on.

You'd better tell me, how does this look?

Susan I'd rather not look at you. It's an element of risk which we really don't need to take. In my experience it is best, it really is best if you always obey the rules.

Lazar But you'd like me to hold on and help you, I think? (*Pause.*) Listen, I'm happy I might be of some use. My own undertaking is somewhat up the spout. Whatever happens I'm several days late. If I could hold on and be of any help . . . I'm sure I'd never have to look you in the face.

Susan All right, if you could just . . .

Lazar Look the opposite . . . yes. I will. I'm delighted. (*He does so.*) All right?

Susan If you could hold on, I'm sure I could find you a bike.

Lazar Would you like a cigarette?

Susan Thank you very much. (*Pause.*) Cafés are bad meeting places, much less safe than they seem. Don't go near Bourges, it's very bad for us. Don't carry anything in toothpaste tubes, it's become the first place they look. Don't laugh too much. An Englishman's laugh, it just doesn't sound the same. Are they still teaching you to broadcast from the lavatory?

Lazar Yes.

Susan Well don't. And don't hide your receiver in the cistern, the whole dodge is badly out of date. The Gestapo have been crashing into lavatories for a full two months. Never take the valley road beyond Poitiers, I'll show you a side road. (*Pause.*) And that's it really. The rest you know, or will learn.

Lazar How long have you been here?

Susan Perhaps a year. Off and on. How's everyone at home?

8

Lazar They're fine.

Susan The boss?

Lazar Fine. Gave me some cufflinks at the aerodrome. Told me my chances.

Susan Fifty-fifty?

Lazar Yes.

Susan He's getting out of touch.

Pause.

Lazar How has it been?

Susan Well . . . the Germans are still here.

Lazar You mean we're failing?

Susan Not at all. It's part of our brief. Keep them here, keep them occupied. Blow up their bridges, devastate the roads, so they have to waste their manpower chasing after us. Divert them from the front. Well, that's what we've done.

Lazar I see.

Susan But it's the worst thing about the job, the more successful you are, the longer it goes on.

Lazar Until we win.

Susan Oh yes. (*Pause.*) A friend . . . a friend who was here used to say, never kill a German, always shoot him in the leg. That way he goes to hospital where he has to be looked after, where he'll use up enemy resources. But a dead soldier is forgotten and replaced.

Pause.

Lazar Do you have dark hair?

Susan What?

9

Lazar One strand across your face. Very young. Sitting one day next to the mahogany door. At the recruitment place. And above your shoulder at the other side, *Whitaker's Almanack*.

Susan turns.

Susan You know who I am.

The sound of an aeroplane. Susan moves back and begins to flash her torch up into the night. Lazar crosses.

Lazar That's it over there.

Susan Wait.

Lazar Isn't that it?

Susan Don't move across. Just wait.

Lazar That's the drop.

The light stops. And the sound of the plane dies. Susan moves back silently and stands behind Lazar looking out into the field.

Susan It's all right, leave it. It's safer to wait a moment or two.

Lazar Oh my God.

Susan What?

Lazar Out across the field. Look . . .

Susan Get down.

They both lie down.

Lazar He's picking it up. Let's get away from here.

Susan No.

Lazar Come on, for God's sake . . .

Susan No.

Lazar If it's the Gestapo . . .

Susan Gestapo nothing, it's the bloody French.

From where they have been looking comes a dark figure running like mad with an enormous parcel wrapped in a parachute. Susan tries to intercept him. A furious row breaks out in heavy whispers.

Posez ça par terre, ce n'est pas à vous.

Frenchman Si, c'est à nous. Je ne vous connais pas.

Susan Non, l'avion était anglais. C'est à nous.

Frenchman Non, c'est désigné pour la résistance.

Lazar Oh God.

He stands watching as Susan, handling the Frenchman very badly, begins to lose her temper. They stand shouting in the night.

Susan Vous savez bien que c'est nous qui devons diriger le mouvement de tous les armements. Pour les français c'est tout à fait impossible . . .

Frenchman Va te faire foutre.

Susan Si vous ne me le donnez pas . . .

Frenchman Les anglais n'ont jamais compris la France. Il faut absolument que ce soit les français qui déterminent notre avenir.

Susan Posez ça . . .

Frenchman C'est pour la France.

The Frenchman begins to go. Lazar has walked quietly across to behind Susan and now takes the gun from her pocket. The Frenchman sees it.

Arr yew raven mad?

Lazar Please put it down. (*Pause.*) Please.

The Frenchman lowers the package to the ground.
Then stands up.

Please tell your friends we're sorry. We do want to help.
Mais parfois ce sont les français mêmes qui le rendent
difficile.

Frenchman Nobody ask you. Nobody ask you to come.
Vous n'êtes pas les bienvenus ici.

Susan is about to reply but Lazar holds up his hand
at once.

Lazar Compris.

Frenchman Espèce de con.

There is a pause. Then the Frenchman turns and walks
out. Lazar keeps him covered, then turns to start
picking the stuff up. Susan moves well away.

Lazar Bloody Gaullists.

Pause.

I mean, what do they have for brains?

Susan I don't know.

Lazar I mean, really.

Susan They just expect the English to die. They sit and
watch us spitting blood in the streets.

Lazar looks up at Susan, catching her tone. Then
moves towards her as calmly as he can.

Lazar Here's your gun.

Lazar slips the gun into Susan's pocket, but as he does
she takes his hand into hers.

We must be off.

Susan I'm sorry, I'm so frightened.

Lazar I must bury the silk.

Susan I'm not an agent, I'm just a courier. I carry messages between certain circuits . . .

Lazar Please . . .

Susan I came tonight, it's my first drop, there is literally nobody else, I can't tell you the mess in Poitiers . . .

Lazar Please.

Susan My friend, the man I mentioned, he's been taken to Buchenwald. He was the wireless operator, please let me tell you, his name was Tony . . .

Lazar I can't help.

Susan I have to talk . . .

Lazar No.

Susan What's the point, what's the point of following the rules if . . .?

Lazar You mustn't . . .

Susan Buchenwald. Do you know what that means?

Lazar Please.

Susan I don't want to die. I don't want to die like that.

Suddenly Susan embraces Lazar, putting her head on his shoulder and crying uncontrollably. He puts his hand through her hair. Then after a long time, she turns and walks some paces away, in silence. They stand for some time.

Lazar Did you know . . . did you know sound waves never die? So every noise we make goes into the sky. And there is a place somewhere in the corner of the universe where all the babble of the world is kept. (*Pause. Then he starts gathering the equipment together.*) Come on, let's clear this lot up. We must be off. I don't know how I'm going to manage on French cigarettes. Is there somewhere I can buy bicycle clips? I was thinking about it all the way down. Oh yes, and something else. A mackerel sky. What is the phrase for that?

Susan Un ciel pommelé.

Lazar Un ciel pommelé. Marvellous. I must find a place to slip it in. Now. Where will I find this bike?

Lazar has collected everything and gone out. Susan follows him.

Susan I don't know your name.

SCENE THREE

Brussels. June 1947.
From the dark the sound of a small string orchestra gives way to the voice of an Announcer.

Announcer Ici Bruxelles – INR. Et maintenant notre soirée continue avec la musique de Victor Silvester et son orchestre. Victor Silvester est parmi les musiciens anglais les plus aimés à cause de ses maintes émissions à la radio anglaise pendant la guerre.

Evening. A gilt room. A fine desk. Good leather chairs. A portrait of the King. Behind the desk Sir Leonard Darwin is working, silver-haired, immaculate, well into his late forties. A knock at the door and Raymond Brock comes in. An ingenuous figure, not yet thirty, with a small moustache and a natural energy he finds hard to contain in the proper manner. He refers constantly to his superior and this makes him uneasy.

Brock Sir Leonard . . .

Darwin Come in.

Brock A few moments of your time. If I could possibly . . .

Darwin You have my ear.

Brock The case of a British national who's died. It's just been landed in my lap. A tourist named Radley's dropped dead in his hotel. It was a coronary, seems fairly clear. The Belgian police took the matter in hand, but naturally the widow has come along to us. It should be quite easy, she's taking it well.

Darwin nods. Brock goes to the door.

Mrs Radley. The ambassador.

Susan has come in. She is simply and soberly dressed. She looks extremely attractive.

Darwin If you'd like to sit down.

She sits opposite him at the desk. Brock stands respectfully at the other side of the room.

Please accept my condolences. The Third Secretary has told me a little of your plight. Naturally we'll help in any way we can.

Brock I've already taken certain practical steps. I've been to the mortuary.

Susan That's very kind.

Brock Belgian undertakers.

Darwin One need not say more. Your husband had a heart attack, is that right?

Susan Yes. In the foyer of our hotel.

Darwin Painless . . .

Susan I would hope. He was packing the car. We were planning to move on this morning. We only have two weeks. We were hoping to make Innsbruck, at least if our travel allowance would last. It was our first holiday since the war.

Darwin Brock, a handkerchief.

Susan No.

Pause.

Brock I was persuaded to opt for an embalming, I'm afraid. It may involve you in some small extra cost.

Susan Excuse me, but you'll have to explain the point.

Brock Sorry?

Susan Of the embalming, I mean.

Brock looks to his superior, but decides to persist.

Brock Well, particularly in the summer, it avoids the possibility of the body exploding at a bad moment. I mean, any moment would be bad, it goes without saying, but on the aeroplane, say.

Susan I see.

Brock You see, normally you find the body's simply washed . . . I don't know how much detail you want me to provide . . .

Darwin I would think it better if . . .

Susan No, I would like to know. Tony was a doctor. He would want me to know.

Brock pauses, then speaks with genuine interest.

Brock To be honest, I was surprised at how little there is to do. There's a small bottle of spirit, colourless, and they simply give the body a wash. The only other thing is the stomach, if there's been a meal, a recent meal . . .

Susan Tony had . . .

Brock Yes, he had breakfast, I think. You insert a pipe into the corpse's stomach to let the gases out. They insert it and there's a strange sort of sigh.

Darwin shifts.

Darwin If, er . . .

Brock It leaves almost no mark. Apparently, so they told me, the morgue attendants, when they're bored, sometimes set light to the gas for a joke. Makes one hell of a bang.

Darwin Shall we all have a drink?

Darwin gets up. Brock tries to backtrack.

Brock But of course I'm sure it didn't happen in this particular case.

Darwin No. There is gin. There is tonic. Yes?

Susan Thank you.

Darwin mixes drinks and hands them round.

Brock I'm afraid we shall need to discuss the practical arrangements. I know the whole subject is very distressing but there is the question . . . you do want the body flown back?

Susan Well, I can hardly stash it in the boot of the car.

A pause. Darwin lost.

Darwin What the Third Secretary is saying . . . not buried on foreign soil.

Susan No.

Brock Quite. You see, for the moment we take care of it, freight charges, and His Majesty's Government picks up the bill. But perhaps later we will have to charge it to the estate, if there is an estate. I'm sorry, I don't mean to interfere . . .

Susan I'm sure there'll be enough to pay for it all. Tony made a very reasonable living.

Darwin Erm . . .

Brock You understand the point.

Susan We'd even talked about the possibility of his death.

Brock Well . . .

Darwin hands Susan a drink.

Susan Thank you. Doctors have a professional life expectancy of the only twenty years. It's a simple fact that most doctors are killed by their patients.

Brock How odd.

Susan Tony was forty-two. It's something of an irony to survive the war, then two years later be destroyed by the rigour of your own profession.

Darwin gets up.

Darwin Well, I think we now understand your needs. I shall go downstairs and set the matter in train.

Brock Would you prefer it if I did that, sir?

Darwin No, no. You stay and talk to Mrs Radley. I'll have a word with the travel people, make a booking on tomorrow morning's flight, if that suits?

Susan Yes, of course.

Darwin You will be going back with the body, I assume?

Susan Yes.

Darwin Are there other dependants? Children?

Susan No.

Darwin goes out. A pause.

Brock If . . .

Susan He doesn't like you.

Brock Sorry.

Susan The ambassador.

Brock Oh. Well, no. (*Pause.*) I don't think he's over the moon about you.

Susan I shouldn't have said that.

Brock No, it's just . . . Darwin thinks disasters are examinations in etiquette. Which fork to use in an earthquake.

Susan Darwin, is that his name?

Brock Yes, the mission all thinks it's God's joke. God getting his own back by dashing off a modern Darwin who is in every aspect less advanced than the last. (*He smiles alone.*) I'm sorry. We sit about in the evenings and polish our jokes. Brussels is rather a debilitating town.

Susan Is this a bad posting for you?

Brock I'd been hoping for something more positive. Fresher air. The flag still flies over a quarter of the human race and I would like to have seen it really. Whereas here . . . we're left with the problems of the war . . . (*He smiles again.*) Have you met any prison governors?

Susan No.

Brock It's just they talk exactly like us. I was hoping for Brixton but I got the Scrubs. Just the same.

Susan Does nobody like it here?

Brock The misery is contagious, I suppose. You spend the day driving between bombsites, watching the hungry, the homeless, the bereaved. We think there are thirty million people loose in Europe who've had to flee across borders, have had to start again. And it is very odd to watch it all from here. (*He gestures round the room.*) Had you been married long?

Susan We met during the war.

Brock I did notice some marks on the body.

Susan Tony was a wireless operator with SOE. Our job was harassment behind the lines. Very successful in Holland, Denmark. Less so in France. Tony was in a circuit the Gestapo destroyed. Then scattered. Ravensbrück, Buchenwald, Saarbrücken, Dachau. Some were tortured, executed.

Brock What did you do?

Susan I was a courier. I was never caught.

She looks straight at Brock.

I wasn't his wife.

Brock No.

Susan Had you realised that?

Brock I'd thought it possible.

Pause.

Susan What about Darwin, did he realise?

Brock Lord, no, it would never occur to him.

Susan Motoring together it was easier to say we were man and wife. In fact I was barely even his mistress. He simply rang me a few weeks ago and asked if I'd like a holiday abroad. I was amazed. People in our organisation really didn't know each other all that well. You made it your business to know as little as possible, it was a point of principle. Even now you don't know who most of your colleagues were. Perhaps you were in it. Perhaps I met you. I don't know. (*Pause.*) Tony I knew a bit better, not much, but I was glad when he rang. Those of us who went through this kind of war, I think we do have something in common. It's a kind of impatience, we're rather intolerant, we don't suffer fools. And so we get rather restless back in England, the people who stayed behind seem childish and a little silly. I think that's why Tony needed to get away. If you haven't suffered . . . well. And so driving through Europe with Tony I knew that at least I'd be able to act as I pleased for a while. That's all. (*Pause.*) It's kind of you not to have told the ambassador.

Brock Perhaps I will. (*He smiles.*) May I ask a question?

Susan Yes.

Brock If you're not his wife, did he have one?

Susan Yes.

Brock I see.

Susan And three children. I had to lie about those, I couldn't claim them somehow. She lives in Crediton in Devon. She believes that Tony was travelling alone. He'd told her he needed two weeks by himself. That's what I was hoping you could do for me.

Brock Ah.

Susan Phone her. I've written the number down. I'm afraid I did it before I came.

Susan opens her handbag and hands across a card. Brock takes it.

Brock And lie?

Susan Yes. I'd prefer it if you lied. But it's up to you.

She looks at Brock. He makes a nervous half-laugh.

All right, doesn't matter . . .

Brock That's not what I said.

Susan Please, it doesn't matter.

Pause.

Brock When did you choose me?

Susan What?

Brock For the job. You didn't choose Darwin.

Susan I might have done.

Pause.

Brock You don't think you wear your suffering a little heavily? This smart club of people you belong to who had a very bad war . . .

Susan All right.

Brock I mean I know it must have put you on a different level from the rest of us . . .

Susan You won't shame me, you know. There's no point. (*Pause.*) It was an innocent relationship. That doesn't mean unphysical. Unphysical isn't innocent. Unphysical in my view is repressed. It just means there was no guilt. I wasn't particularly fond of Tony, he was very slow-moving and egg-stained, if you know what I mean, but we'd known some sorrow together and I came with him. And so it seemed a shocking injustice when he fell in the lobby, unjust for him of course, but also unjust for me, alone, a long way from home, and worst of all for his wife, bitterly unfair if she had to have the news from me. Unfair for life. And so I approached the embassy. (*Pause.*)

Obviously I shouldn't even have mentioned the war. Tony used to say, don't talk about it. He had a dread of being trapped in small rooms with big Jewish women, I know exactly what he meant. I should have just come here this evening and sat with my legs apart, pretended to be a scarlet woman, then at least you would have been able to place me. It makes no difference. Lie or don't lie. It's a matter of indifference.

Brock gets up and moves uncertainly around the room. Susan stays where she is.

Brock Would you . . . perhaps I could ask you to dinner? Just so we could talk . . .

Susan No. I refuse to tell you anything now. If I told you anything about myself you would just think I was pleading, that I was trying to get round you. So I tell you nothing. I just say look at me – don't creep round the furniture – look at me and make a judgement.

Brock Well.

Darwin reappears. He picks up his drink and sits at his desk as if to clear up. There is in fact nothing to clear up, so mostly he just moves his watch round. He talks the while.

Darwin That's done. First flight tomorrow without a hitch.

Brock stands as if unaware Darwin has come back.

Susan Thank you very much.

Darwin If there's anything else. There is a small chapel in the embassy if you'd like to use it before you go.

Susan Thank you.

Brock turns and walks abruptly out of the room. Susan smiles a moment. Darwin puts on his watch.

Have you been posted here long?

Darwin No, not at all. Just a few months. Before that, Djakarta. We were hoping for something sunny but Brussels came along. Not that we're complaining. They've certainly got something going here.

Susan Really?

Darwin Oh yes. New Europe. Yes yes. (*Pause.*) Reconstruction. Massive. Massive work of reconstruction. Jobs. Ideals. Marvellous. Marvellous time to be alive in Europe. No end of it. Roads to be built. People to be educated. Land to be tilled. Lots to get on with. (*Pause.*) Have another gin.

Susan No thanks.

Darwin The diplomat's eye is the clearest in the world. Seen from Djakarta this continent looks so old, so beautiful. We don't realise what we have in our hands.

Susan No.

Brock reappears at the door.

Brock Your wife is asking if you're ready for dinner, sir.

Darwin Right.

Brock And she wants your advice on her face.

Darwin gets up.

I'll lock up after you, sir.

Darwin You'll see Mrs Radley to her hotel?

Brock Of course.

Darwin Goodbye, Mrs Radley. I'm sorry it hasn't been a happier day.

Darwin goes out. Brock closes the door. He looks at Susan.

Brock I've put in a call to England. There's an hour's delay. (*Pause.*) I've decided to lie.

Brock and Susan stare at each other. Silence.

Will you be going back with the body?

Susan No.

Brock goes to the door and listens. Then turns back and removes his buttonhole. He looks for somewhere to put it. He finds his undrunk gin and tonic and puts it in there. Then he takes his jacket off and drops it somewhat deliberately on the floor. He takes a couple of paces towards Susan.

Brock Will you remind me to cancel your seat?

SCENE FOUR

Pimlico. September 1947.

From the dark the sound of a string quartet. It comes to an end. Then a voice.

Announcer This is the BBC Third Programme. Vorichef wrote *Les Ossifiés* in the year of the Paris Commune, but his struggle with Parkinson's disease during the writing of the score has hitherto made it a peculiarly difficult manuscript for musicologists to interpret. However the leader of the Bremen Ensemble has recently done a magnificent work of reclamation. Vorichef died in an extreme state of senile dementia in 1878. This performance of his last work will be followed by a short talk in our series 'Musicians and Disease'.

A bed-sitter with some wooden chairs, a bed and a canvas bed with a suitcase set beside it. A small room, well maintained but cheerless. Alice sits on the floor in a chalk-striped men's suit and white tie. She smokes a hookah.

   Susan is on the edge of the bed drinking cocoa. She is wearing a blue striped shirt. Her revolver lies beside her. Brock is laid out fast asleep across two chairs in his pinstripes. Next to him is a large pink parcel, an odd item of luxury in the dismal surroundings. By the way they talk you know it's late.

Susan I want to move on. I do desperately want to feel I'm moving on.

Alice With him?

Susan Well that's the problem, isn't it?

   Pause. Alice smiles.

Alice You are strange.

Susan Well, what would you do?

Alice I'd trade him in.

Susan Would you?

Alice I'd choose someone else off the street.

Susan And what chance would you have tonight, within a mile, say, within a mile of here?

Alice Let me think. Does that take in Victoria Bus Station?

Susan No.

Alice Then pretty slim.

Susan Is that right?

   They smile. The hookah smokes.

That thing is disgusting.

Alice I know. It was better when the dung was fresh.

Susan I don't know why you bother . . .

Alice The writer must experience everything, every kind of degradation. Nothing is closed to him. It's really the degradation that attracted me to the job.

Susan I thought you were going to work tonight . . .

Alice I can't write all the time. You have to live it before you can write it. What other way is there? Besides nicking it.

Susan Is that done?

Alice Apparently. Once you start looking it seems most books are copied out of other books. Only it's called tribute. Tribute to Hemingway. Means it's nicked. Mine's going to be tribute to Scott Fitzgerald. Have you read him?

Susan No.

Alice *Last Tycoon.* Mine's going to be like that. Not quite the same of course. Something of a bitch to make Ealing Broadway hum like Hollywood Boulevard but otherwise it's in the bag.

Brock grunts.

He snores.

Susan You should get a job.

Alice I've had a job, I know what jobs are like. Had a job in your office.

Susan For three days.

Alice It was enough.

Susan How are you going to live?

Alice Off you mostly. (*She smiles.*) Susan . . .

Susan I want to move on. I do desperately want to feel I'm moving on. (*Pause.*) I work so hard I have no time to think. The office is worse. Those brown invoices go back and forth, import, export . . .

Alice I remember.

Susan They get heavier and heavier as the day goes on, I can barely stagger across the room for the weight of a single piece of paper, by the end of the day if you dropped one on the floor, you would smash your foot. The silence is worse. Dust gathering. Water lapping beyond the wall. It seems unreal. You can't believe that because of the work you do ships pass and sail across the world. (*She stares a moment.*) Mr Medlicott has moved into my office.

Alice Frightful Mr Medlicott?

Susan Yes.

Alice The boss?

Susan He has moved in. Or rather, more sinister still, he has removed the frosted glass between our two offices.

Alice Really?

Susan I came in one morning and found the partition had gone. I interpret it as the first step in a mating dance. I believe Medlicott stayed behind one night, set his ledger aside, ripped off his tweed suit and his high collar, stripped naked, took up an axe, swung it at the partition, dropped to the floor, rolled over in the broken glass till he bled, till his whole body streamed blood, then he cleared up, slipped home, came back next morning and waited to see if anything would be said. But I have said nothing. And neither has he. He puts his head down and does not lift it till lunch. I have to look across at his few strands of hair, like seaweed across his skull. And I am frightened of what the next step will be.

Alice I can imagine.

Susan The sexual pressure is becoming intolerable.

They smile.

One day there was a condom in his turn-up. Used or unused I couldn't say. But planted without a doubt. Again, nothing said. I tried to laugh it off to myself, pretended he'd been off with some whore in Limehouse and not bothered to take his trousers off, so that after the event the condom had just absent-mindedly fallen from its place and lodged alongside all the bus tickets and the tobacco and the raisins and the paper-clips and all the rest of it. But I know the truth. It was step two. And the dance has barely begun. (*Pause.*) Alice. I must get out.

Alice Then do. Just go. Have you never done that? I do it all the time.

Susan They do need me in that place.

Alice So much the better, gives it much more point. That's always the disappointment when I leave, I always go before people even notice I've come. But you . . . you could really make a splash.

Brock stirs.

He stirs.

Susan I'd like to change everything but I don't know how.

She leans under her bed, pulls out a shoebox, starts to oil and clean her gun.

Alice Are you really fond of him?

Susan You don't see him at his best. We had a week in Brussels which we both enjoyed. Now he comes over for the weekend whenever he can. But he tends to be rather sick on the boat.

Alice You should meet someone younger.

Susan That's not what I mean. And I don't really like young men. You're through and out the other side in no time at all.

Alice I can introduce you . . .

Susan I'm sure. I've only known you three weeks, but I've got the idea. Your flair for agonised young men. I think you get them in bulk from tuberculosis wards.

Alice I'm just catching up, that's all.

Susan Of course.

Alice I was a late starter.

Susan Oh yes, what are you, eighteen?

Alice I started late. Out of guilt. I had a protected childhood. Till I ran away. And very bad guilt. I was frightened to masturbate more than once a week, I thought my clitoris was like a torch battery, you know, use it too much and it runs out.

Brock wakes.

He wakes.

They watch as he comes round.

Brock What time is it?

Alice Raymond, can you give us your view? I was just comparing the efficiency of a well-known household object with . . .

Susan Alice, leave him alone.

Alice It's getting on for five.

Brock I feel terrible.

Susan (*kissing his head*) I'll get you something to eat. Omelette all right? It's only powder, I'm afraid . . .

Brock Well . . .

Susan Two spoons or three? And I'll sprinkle it with Milk of Magnesia. (*She goes out into the kitchen.*)

Brock It seems a bit pointless. It's only twelve hours till I'm back on the boat. (*He picks up the gun.*) Did I miss something?

Alice No. She's just fondling it.

Brock Ah.

He looks round. Alice is watching him all the time.

I can't remember what . . .

Alice Music. On the wireless. You had us listening to some music.

Brock Ah, that's right.

Alice Some composer who shook.

Brock I thought you'd have gone. Don't you have a flat?

Alice I did. But it had bad associations. I was disappointed in love.

Brock I see.

Alice And Susan said I could sleep here.

Brock (*absently admiring her suit*) I must say I do think your clothes are very smart.

Alice Well, I tell you he looks very good in mine. (*She nods at the parcel.*) Do you always bring her one of those?

Brock I certainly try to bring a gift if I can.

Alice You must have lots of money.

Brock Well, I suppose. I find it immoderately easy to acquire. I seem to have a sort of mathematical gift. The

31

stock exchange. Money sticks to my fingers, I find. I triple my income. What can I do?

Alice It must be very tiresome.

Brock Oh . . . I'm acclimatising, you know. (*Smiles.*) I think everyone's going to be rich very soon. Once we've got over the effects of war. It's going to be coming out of everyone's ears.

Alice Is that what you think?

Brock I'm absolutely sure. (*Pause.*) I do enjoy these weekends, you know. Susan leads such an interesting life. Books. Conversation. People like you. The Foreign Office can make you feel pretty isolated – also, to be honest, make you feel pretty small, as if you're living on sufferance, you can imagine . . .

Alice Yes.

Brock Till I met Susan. The very day I met her, she showed me you must always do what you want. If you want something you must get it. I think that's a wonderful way to live, don't you?

Alice I do. (*Pause. She smiles.*) Shall I tell you how my book begins?

Brock Well . . .

Alice There's a woman in a rape trial. And the story is true. The book begins at the moment where she has to tell the court what the accused has said to her on the night of the rape. And she finds she can't bring herself to say the words out loud. And so the judge suggests she writes them down on a piece of paper and it be handed round the court. Which she does. And it says, 'I want to have you. I must have you now.' (*She smiles again.*) So they pass it round the jury who all read it and pass it on. At the end of the second row there's a woman jurist who's fallen asleep at the boredom of the trial. So the man next to her has to nudge her awake and hand her the slip of paper. She wakes up, looks at it, then at him, smiles and puts it in her handbag. (*She laughs.*) That woman is my heroine.

Brock Well, yes.

Susan returns, sets food on Brock's knee. Then returns to cleaning her gun. Alice tries to re-light her hookah.

Susan Cheese omelette. What were you talking about?

Alice The rape trial.

Susan Did you tell Raymond who the woman was?

Brock What do you mean?

Susan I'm only joking, dear.

Alice and Susan laugh.

Brock I'm not sure it's the sort of . . .

Alice Oh sod this stuff.

Susan I said it was dung.

Alice I was promised visions.

Brock Well . . .

Alice It's because I'm the only Bohemian in London. People exploit me. Because there are no standards, you see. In Paris or New York, there are plenty of Bohemians, so the kief is rich and sweet and plentiful but here . . . you'd be better off to lick the gum from your ration card.

Susan Perhaps Raymond will be posted to Morocco, bring some back in his bag . . .

Brock I don't think that's really on.

Susan Nobody would notice, from what you say. Nobody would notice if you smoked it yourself.

Alice Are they not very sharp?

Susan Not according to Raymond. The ones I've met are buffoons . . .

Brock Susan, please . . .

Susan Well, it's you who call them buffoons.

Brock It's not quite what I say.

Susan It's you who tell the stones. That man Darwin . . .

Brock Please . . .

Susan How he needs three young men from public schools to strap him into his surgical support.

Brock I told you that in confidence.

Susan In gloves.

Alice Really?

Brock Darwin is not a buffoon.

Susan From your own lips . . .

Brock He just has slight problems of adjustment to the modern age.

Susan You are laughing.

Brock I am not laughing.

Susan There is a slight smile at the corner of your mouth . . .

Brock There is not. There is absolutely no smile.

Susan Alice, I will paraphrase, let me paraphrase Raymond's view of his boss. I don't misrepresent you, dear, it is, in paraphrase, in sum, that he would not trust him to stick his prick into a bucket of lard.

Brock puts his omelette to one side, uneaten.

Well, is he a joke or is he not?

Brock Certainly he's a joke.

Susan Thank you.

Brock He's a joke between us. He is not a joke to the entire world. (*A pause. He looks at Alice. Then he gets up.*) I think I'd better be pushing off home.

Brock goes and gets his coat. Puts it on. Susan at least speaks, very quietly.

Susan And I wish you wouldn't use those words.

Brock What?

Susan Words like 'push off home'. You're always saying it. 'Bit of a tight corner', 'one hell of a spot'. They don't belong.

Brock What do you mean?

Susan They are not your words.

Pause.

Brock Well, I'm none too keen on your words either.

Susan Oh yes, which?

Brock The words you've been using this evening.

Susan Such as?

Brock You know perfectly well.

Susan Such as, come on, tell me, what words have I used?

Brock Words like . . . (*Pause.*) Bucket of lard.

Pause.

Susan Alice, there is only the bath or the kitchen.

Alice I know.

Alice goes out. Susan automatically picks up the omelette and starts to eat it.

Brock Are you going to let her live with you?

Susan I like her. She makes me laugh.

Pause.

Brock I'm sorry, I was awful, I apologise. But the work I do is not entirely contemptible. Of course our people are dull, they're stuffy, they're death. But what other world do I have?

Pause.

Susan I think of France more than I tell you. I was seventeen and I was thrown into the war. I often think of it.

Brock I'm sure.

Susan The most unlikely people. People I met only for an hour or two. Astonishing kindnesses. Bravery. The fact you could meet someone for an hour or two and see the very best of them and then move on. Can you understand?

Pause. Brock does not move.

For instance, there was a man in France. His codename was Lazar. I'd been there a year, I suppose, and one night I had to see him on his way. He just dropped out of the sky. An agent. He was lost. I was trying to be blasé, trying to be tough, all the usual stuff – irony, hardness, cleverness, wit – and then suddenly I began to cry. On to the shoulder of a man I'd never met before. But not a day goes by without my wondering where he is.

Susan finishes her omelette and puts the plate aside. Brock moves towards her.

Brock Susan.

Susan I think we should try a winter apart. I really do. I think it's all a bit easy this way. These weekends. Nothing is tested. I think a test would be good. Then we would know. And what better test than a winter apart?

Brock A winter together.

Pause. They smile.

Susan I would love to come to Brussels, you know that. I would love to come if it weren't for my job. But the shipping office is very important to me. I do find it fulfilling. And I just couldn't let Mr Medlicott down. (*Pause.*) You must say what you think.

Brock looks at Susan hard, then shrugs and smiles.

I know you've been dreading the winter crossings, high seas . . .

Brock Don't patronise me, Susan.

Susan Anyway, perhaps in the spring, it would be really nice to meet . . .

Brock Please don't insult my intelligence. I know you better than you think. I recognise the signs. When you talk longingly about the war . . . some deception usually follows. (*He kisses Susan.*) Goodbye.

Brock goes out. Susan left standing for a few moments. Then she picks up the plate and goes quickly to the kitchen. Alice comes out of the bathroom at once in a dressing-gown. She has a notebook in her hand which she tosses the length of the room, so it lands on a chair. She settles on her back in the camp bed. Susan reappears at the door.

Susan Did you hear that?

Alice Certainly. I was writing it down.

Susan looks across at her, but Alice is putting pennies on her eyes.

My death-mask.

Susan Don't.

Alice I dream better.

Pause.

Susan Do you know what you're doing tomorrow?

Alice Not really. There's a new jazz band at the One-O-One. And Ken wants to take me to Eel Pie Island in his horrid little car. I say I'll go if I get to meet Alistair. I really do want to meet Alistair. Everyone says he's got hair on his shoulder-blades and apparently he can crack walnuts in his armpits.

Susan Oh well, he'll never be short of friends.

Alice Quite.

Susan turns out one light. Dim light only. She looks at the parcel.

Susan What should I be doing with this?

Alice If we can't eat it, let's throw it away.

Susan turns out the other light. Darkness. The sound of Susan getting into bed.

Your friend Brock says we're all going to be rich.

Susan Oh really?

Pause.

Alice Peace and plenty.

SCENE FIVE

Temple. May 1951.

Music, a cello leading. The Embankment, beside a lamp, overlooking the river.

Night. Susan stands, thickly wrapped. For the first time, she is expensively dressed. She is eating hot chestnuts. Mick appears at the back. He is from the East End. He looks twenty, smart and personable. He speaks before she knows he's there.

Mick Five hundred cheese-graters.

Susan Oh no.

Mick I got five hundred cheese-graters parked round the side. Are you interested?

Susan I'm afraid you're too late. We took a consignment weeks ago.

Susan laughs. Mick moves down beside her.

Mick Where we looking?

Susan Across the river. Over there.

Mick Where?

Susan South Bank. That's where the fireworks are going to be. And there's my advertising balloon.

Mick Oh yeah. What does it say?

Susan Don't say that, that's the worst thing you can say.

Mick It's dark.

Susan It says 'Bovril'.

Mick Oh, Bovril.

Susan Yes. It's meant to blaze out over London.

Mick Surprised it hasn't got your name on.

Susan What do you mean?

Mick Everywhere I go.

Pause. They look at each other. Susan smiles and removes a napkin from her coat pocket, and unfolds its bundle.

Susan I managed to steal some supper from the Festival Hall. There's a réception for its opening night. They're using your cutlery, I'm happy to say.

Mick I wish I could see it.

Susan Yes, yes, I wish you could too. (*She smiles.*) I've actually decided to leave the Festival now. Having worked so hard to get the wretched thing on. I'm thinking of going into advertising.

Mick Ah, very good.

Susan I met some people on the Bovril side. It's . . . well, I doubt if it'll stretch me, but it would be a way of having some fun. (*Pause.*) Would you like a canapé?

Mick How's Alice?

Susan She's very well.

Mick Haven't seen her lately.

Susan No.

Mick She went mainstream, you see. I stayed revivalist. Different religion. For me jazz stopped dead in 1919.

He takes a canapé.

So how can I help?

Susan I'm looking for a father. I want to have a child. (*Pause.*) Look, it really is much easier than it sounds. I mean, marriage is not involved. Or even looking after it. You don't even have to see the pregnancy through. I mean, conception will be the end of the job.

Mick smiles.

Mick Ah.

Susan You don't want to?

Mick No, no, I'm delighted, I'm lucky to be asked.

Susan Not at all.

Mick But it's just . . . your own people. I mean friends, you must have friends.

Susan It's . . .

Mick I mean . . .

Susan Sorry.

Mick No, go on, say.

Susan The men I know at work, at the Festival, or even friends I've known for years, they just aren't the kind of people I would want to marry.

Mick Ah.

Susan I'm afraid I'm rather strong-minded, as you know, and so with them I usually feel I'm holding myself in for fear of literally blowing them out of the room. They are kind, they are able, but I don't see . . . why I should have to compromise, why I should have to make some sad and decorous marriage just to have a child. I don't see why any woman should have to do that.

Mick But you don't have to marry . . .

Susan Ah well . . .

Mick Just go off with them.

41

Susan But that's really the problem. These same men, these kind and likeable men, they do have another side to their nature and that is they are very limited in their ideas, they are frightened of the unknown, they want a quiet life where sex is either sport or duty but absolutely nothing in between, and they simply would not agree to sleep with me if they knew it was a child I was after.

Mick But you wouldn't have to tell them.

Susan I did think that. But then I thought it would be dishonest. And so I had the idea of asking a person whom I barely knew.

Pause.

Mick What about the kid?

Susan What?

Mick Doesn't sound a very good deal. Never to see his dad . . .

Susan It's not . . .

Mick I take it that is what you mean.

Susan I think it's what I mean.

Mick Well?

Susan The child will manage.

Mick How do you know?

Susan Being a bastard won't always be so bad.

Mick I wouldn't bet on it.

Susan England can't be like this for ever.

Mick looks at her.

Mick I would like to know . . .

Susan Yes?

Mick Why you chose me. I mean, how often have you met me?

Susan Yes, but that's the whole point . . .

Mick With Alice a few times . . .

Susan And you sold me some spoons.

Mick They were good spoons.

Susan I'm not denying it.

Mick smiles.

Mick And Alice says what? That I'm clean and obedient and don't have any cretins in the family?

Susan It's not as calculated as that.

Mick Not calculated? Several hundred of us, was there, all got notes . . .

Susan No.

Mick . . . saying come and watch the Festival fireworks, tell no one, bring no friends. All the secrecy, I thought you must at least be after nylons . . .

Susan I'll buy nylons. If that's what you want.

They stare at each other.

Mick So why me?

Susan I like you.

Mick And?

Susan 'I love you'? (*Pause.*) I chose you because . . . I don't see you very much. I barely ever see you. We live at opposite ends of town. Different worlds.

Mick Different class.

Susan That comes into it.

There is a pause. Mick looks at her. Then moves away. Turns back. Smiles.

Mick Oh dear.

Susan Then laugh. (*Pause.*) I never met the man I wanted to marry.

They smile.

Mick It can't be what you want. Not deep down.

Susan No.

Mick I didn't think so.

Susan Deep down I'd do the whole damn thing by myself. But there we are. You're second-best.

They smile again.

Mick Five hundred cheese-graters.

Susan How much?

Mick Something over the odds. A bit over the odds. Not much.

Susan Done. (*Pause.*) Don't worry. The Festival will pay.

Susan moves across to Mick. They kiss. They look at each other. He smiles. Then they turn and look at the night. He is barely audible.

Mick Fireworks. If you . . .

Susan What?

Mick Stay for the fireworks.

Susan If you like.

Pause.

Mick Great sky.

Susan Yes.

Mick The light. Those dots.

Susan A mackerel sky.

Mick Say?

Susan That's what they call it. A mackerel sky.

SCENE SIX

Pimlico. December 1952.

From the dark the sound of Charlie Parker and his saxophone.

Night. The bed-sitting room transformed. The beds have gone and the room is much more comfortable. Three people. Susan is working at her desk which is covered with papers and drawings. Alice is standing over a table which has been cleared so that she may paint the naked body of Louise who lies stretched across its top. She is in her late teens, from Liverpool. Alice is a good way on with the job. The record ends.

Susan This is hell.

Alice No doubt.

Susan I am living in hell.

Susan sits back and stares at her desk. Alice goes to the record player.

Alice Shall we hear it again?

Susan You're only allowed it once. Hear it too much and you get out of hand.

Alice It's true. (*She turns it off and returns to painting.*) I'd give that up if I were you. We have to go pretty soon.

Susan Why do I lie?

Alice We have to get there by midnight.

Susan What do I do it for?

Alice It's your profession.

Susan That's what's wrong. In France . . .

Alice Ah, France.

Susan I told such glittering lies. But where's the fun in lying for a living?

Alice What's today's?

Susan Some leaking footwear. Some rotten shoe I have to advertise. What is the point? Why do I exist?

Alice Sold out.

Susan Sold out. Is that the phrase?

Pause. Alice paints. Susan stares.

Prostitution. Shame. And decay.

Alice Turn over, let me do the other side.

Louise moves on to her stomach.

Susan To produce what my masters call good copy, it is simply a question of pitching my intelligence low enough. Shutting my eyes and imagining what it's like to be very, very stupid. This is all the future holds for any of us. We will spend the next twenty years of our lives pretending to be thick. 'I'm sorry, Miss Traherne, we'd like to employ you, but unfortunately you are not stupid enough.'

Susan tears up the work she is doing and sits back glaring. Alice explains to Louise.

Alice You're all trunk up to here, OK?

46

Louise Yeah, right.

Alice The trunk is all one, so you just have to keep your legs together. Then you break into leaf, just above the bust.

Louise Do I get conkers?

Alice No. If you were a chestnut, you'd get conkers. But you're an oak.

Louise What does an oak have?

Alice An oak has acorns.

Louise Acorns?

Alice But you won't need them, I promise. We scorn gimmicks. We will win as we are.

Susan (*to herself*) The last night of the year . . .

Alice And I will sell a great many paintings. (*Pause. She paints.*) Louise is staying with Emma and Willy . . .

Susan Oh yes?

Louise I met them in the street, I'd just left home, come down the A6.

Susan Good for you.

Louise I couldn't believe my luck.

Alice Willy's going as a kipper, I do know that. And Emma's a prostitute, though how we're meant to know it's fancy dress I really can't think.

Louise I've gathered that.

Alice Otherwise I expect the usual historical riff-raff. Henry VIII, that sort of thing. We ought to walk it with a naked oak.

Louise Will that friend of yours be there?

A moment. Susan looks across at Alice and Louise.

Alice No. He'll be tucked up with his syphilitic wife.

Louise Why doesn't he . . . ?

Susan Shut up, Louise.

Alice It's all right. Ask what you want.

Pause.

Louise How do you know she's syphilitic?

Alice How do you think? She passed it down the line.

Louise Oh God.

Alice Or somebody passed it and I've decided to blame her. It seems right somehow. She's a very plausible incubator for a social disease. Back over.

Louise turns again.

Louise Why doesn't he leave?

Alice Who?

Louise Your friend.

Alice Ah well, if they ever did leave their wives, perhaps the whole sport would die. For all of us.

Susan Roll on 1953.

Alice smiles and resumes painting.

Alice Actually the clinic say it's non-specific urethritis, which I find rather insulting. I did at least expect the doctor to come out and apologise and say, I'm sorry not to be more specific about your urethritis, but no, they just leave you in the air.

As she is talking Mick has appeared at the door.

Mick I wonder, does anyone mind if I come in?

Alice Mick?

Mick moves into the room.

Mick Would you mind if I . . . ?

Susan How did you get this address?

Alice Do you two know each other?

Mick Happy New Year.

Pause.

Alice Mick, may I introduce you to Louise?

Louise Hello, Mick.

Mick Hello, Louise.

Alice Louise is going to the Arts Ball, I'm painting her . . .

Mick Ah.

Alice She's going as a tree.

Susan Mick, I really don't want to talk to you.

Alice What's wrong?

Mick Is she really going to walk down the street . . .

Susan I thought we'd agreed. You promised me, Mick. You made a promise. Never to meet again.

A pause. Mick looks down.

Mick I just thought . . . well, it's New Year's Eve and well . . . one or two weeks have gone by . . .

Susan Have you been watching the house? Is that how you found me? Have you been following me home? (*She stares across at him.*) Mick, I think you'd better sit over there and you will tell us exactly why you've come.

Pause.

Louise Does anyone mind if I put my clothes on?

They ignore her.

Susan I am in no mood for it, Mick. I really did leave it all behind the last time I saw you on whatever building site or dumptruck that was . . .

Mick Look, all I want is . . .

Susan Leave it, just leave it where it is.

Mick I can't.

There is a pause. Louise has swung down from the table, but now stands staring at them. Then in the silence she picks up her clothes and goes into the kitchen. Alice speaks much more quietly.

Alice She's not finished. She'll look good when it's done.

Pause.

Susan I asked Mick to father a child, that's what we're talking about.

Mick Oh Christ.

Susan Well, we have tried over eighteen months, that's right? And we have failed.

Mick Right.

Susan Which leaves us both feeling pretty stupid, pretty wretched, I would guess, speaking for myself. And there is a point of decency at which the experiment should stop.

Mick Susan . . .

Susan We have nothing in common, never did, that was part of the idea . . .

Mick It just feels bad . . .

Susan The idea was fun, it was simple, it depended on two adults behaving like adults.

Mick It feels very bad to be used.

Susan I would have stopped it months ago, I would have stopped it in the second month . . .

Mick You come out feeling dirty.

Susan And how do I feel? What am I meant to feel? Crawling about in your tiny bedroom, paper-thin walls, your mother sitting downstairs . . .

Mick Don't bring my mum into this.

Susan Scrabbling about on bombsites, you think I enjoy all that?

Mick Yeah. Very much. I think you do.

Pause. Alice looks away. Susan moves quietly away as if to give it up. Mick calms down.

I just think . . .

Susan I know what you think. You think I enjoy slumming around. Then why have I not looked for another father? Because the whole exploit has broken my heart.

Pause.

Mick You think it's my fault.

Susan Oh Lord, is that all you're worried about?

Mick You think it's something to do with me?

Susan That was part of it, never to have to drag through this kind of idiot argument . . .

Mick Well, it is quite important.

Susan You don't understand. You don't understand the figures in my mind. (*Pause.*) Mick, there is gentlemen's footwear. It must be celebrated. I have to find words to convey the sensation of walking round London on two pieces of reconstituted cardboard stuck together with horseglue. And I have to find them tonight.

Susan goes to her desk, takes out fresh paper. Starts work. Louise comes from the kitchen, plainly dressed.

Louise I'll tell the others. You may be late.

Alice stoops down and picks up a couple of papier-mâché green branches.

Alice There are some branches. You have to tie them round your wrists.

Louise Thanks all the same. I'll just go as myself.

Louise goes out. There is a silence, as Susan works at her desk. Alice sits with her hand over her eyes. Mick sits miserably staring. This goes on for some time until finally Susan speaks very quietly, without looking up from her desk.

Susan Mick, will you go now please?

Mick You people are cruel.

Susan Please.

Mick You are cruel and dangerous.

Susan Mick.

Mick You fuck people up. This little tart and her string of married men, all fucked up, all fucking ruined by this tart. And you . . . and you . . .

Mick turns to Susan. Susan gets up and walks quietly from the room. A pause. Alice is looking at him.

She is actually mad.

Susan reappears with her revolver. She fires it just over Mick's head. It is deafeningly loud. He falls to the ground. She fires three more times.

Mick Jesus Christ.

SCENE SEVEN

Knightsbridge. October 1956.
From the dark, music, emphatic, triumphant.
The room we saw in Scene One. But now decorated with heavy velvet curtains, china objects and soft furniture. A diplomatic home. Both men in dinner-jackets: Brock smokes a cigar and drinks brandy. Opposite him is an almost permanently smiling Burmese, M. Aung, short, dogmatic. The music stops.

Aung Two great nations, sir. The Americans and the English. Like the Romans and the Greeks. Americans are the Romans – power, armies, strength. The English are the Greeks – ideas civilisation, intellect. Between them they shall rule the world.

Darwin appears putting his head round the door. He is also in a dinner-jacket. He appears exhausted.

Darwin Good Lord, I hope you haven't hung on for me.

Brock Leonard, come in, how kind of you to come.

Darwin Not at all.

Brock ushers him in. Aung stands.

Brock Our little gathering. We'd scarcely dared hope . . .

Darwin There seemed nothing left to do.

Brock Leonard, you know M. Aung, of course?

Aung Mr Darwin.

Darwin Rangoon.

Brock Now First Secretary, Burmese Embassy.

Aung An honour. A privilege. A moment in my career. I shake your hand. (*He does so.*)

Darwin Good, good. Well . . .

Brock Let me get you a drink.

Darwin That would be very kind.

Brock I'll just tell my wife you're here.

Brock goes out. Aung smiles at Darwin.

Aung Affairs of state?

Darwin Yes, if you . . .

Aung Say no more. We have eaten. We did not wait. In Burma we say if you cannot be on time, do not come at all.

Darwin Really?

Aung But of course the English it is different. At your command the lion makes its bed with the lamb.

Darwin Hardly.

Aung Don't worry. All will be well. Ah, Darwin of Djakarta, to have met the man, to have been alone with him. I shall dine in on this for many years.

Darwin Dine out on this.

Aung Ah, the English language, she is a demanding mistress, yes?

Darwin If you like.

Aung And no one controls her so well as you, sir. You beat her and the bitch obeys. (*He laughs.*) The language of the world. Good, good. I have learnt the phrase from you. Out of your mouth. Good, good. I am behind you, sir.

Susan appears in a superbly cut evening dress. She is dangerously cheerful. Brock follows her.

Susan Leonard, how good of you to make an appearance.

Darwin I'm only sorry I've been delayed.

Susan and Darwin kiss.

Susan Brock says you're all ragged with fatigue. I hear you've been having the most frightful week . . .

Darwin It has been, yes.

Susan Well, don't worry. Here at least you can relax. You've met Mr Aung?

Darwin Indeed.

Susan You can forget everything. The words 'Suez Canal' will not be spoken.

Darwin That will be an enormous relief.

Susan They are banned, you will not hear them.

Darwin Thank you, my dear.

Susan Nasser, nobody will mention his name.

Darwin Quite.

Susan Nobody will say 'blunder' or 'folly' or 'fiasco'. Nobody will say 'international laughing stock'. You are among friends, Leonard. I will rustle up some food.

She smiles at Aung.

Mr Aung, I think the gentlemen may wish to talk.

Aung Of course, in such company I am privileged to change sex. (*He gets up to follow Susan out.*)

Susan Nobody will say 'death-rattle of the ruling class'. We have stuck our lips together with marron glacé. I hope you understand.

Susan and Aung go out. Pause.

Brock Sorry, I . . .

Darwin It's all right.

Brock I did ask her to calm down.

Darwin I'm getting used to it.

Brock She's been giving me hell. She knows how closely you've been involved . . .

Darwin Do you think we could leave the subject, Brock? (*Pause.*) I'm eager for the drink.

Brock Of course.

Darwin At least she got rid of that appalling wog. I mean, in honesty, Raymond, what are you trying to do to me?

Brock I'm sorry, sir.

Darwin This week of all weeks. He had his tongue stuck so far up my fundament all you could see of him were the soles of his feet.

Brock takes over a tray of drinks.

Mental illness, is it? Your wife?

Brock No, she just . . . feels very strongly. Well, you know . . .

Darwin But there has been mental illness?

Brock In the past.

Darwin Yes?

Brock Before we were married. Some years ago. She'd been living very foolishly, a loose set in Pimlico. And a series of jobs, pushing herself too hard. Not eating. We got engaged when she was still quite ill, and I have tried to help her back up.

Darwin That's very good.

Brock Well . . .

Darwin Second marriage, of course. Often stabilises.

Brock What?

Darwin The chap in Brussels. (*Pause.*) The stiff.

Brock Ah yes.

Darwin You don't have to be ashamed . . .

Brock No, I'm not, it's . . .

Darwin In the diplomatic service it isn't as if a mad wife is any kind of professional disadvantage. On the contrary, it almost guarantees promotion.

Brock Well . . .

Darwin Some of the senior men, their wives are absolutely barking. I take the word 'gouache' to be the giveaway. When they start drifting out of rooms saying, 'I think I'll just go and do my gouaches, dear,' then you know you've lost them for good and all.

Brock But Susan isn't mad.

Darwin No, no. (*Pause.*) Is there a Madame Aung?

Brock In the other room.

Darwin I knew there had to be. Somehow. And no doubt culturally inclined. Traditional dance, she'll tell us about, in the highlands of Burma. Or the plot of *Lohengrin.*

Brock Leonard . . .

Darwin I'm sorry. I think I've had it, Brock. One more Aung and I throw in the can.

Pause.

Do you mind if I have a cherry?

Brock What?

Darwin The maraschinos. I'm so hungry. It's all those bloody drugs we have to take.

Brock Let me . . .

Darwin Stay. (*Pause.*) We have been betrayed. (*He reaches into the cocktail cherries with his fingers, but then just rolls them slowly in his palm.*) We claim to be intervening as a neutral party in a dispute between Israel and Egypt. Last Monday the Israelis launched their attack. On Tuesday we issued our ultimatum saying both sides must withdraw to either side of the canal. But, Raymond, the Israelis, the aggressors, they were nowhere near the canal. They'd have had to advance a hundred miles to make the retreat.

Brock Who told you that?

Darwin Last week the Foreign Secretary went abroad. I was not briefed. We believe he met with the French and the Israelis, urged the Israelis to attack. I believe our ultimatum was written in France last week, hence the mistake in the wording. The Israelis had reckoned to reach the canal, but met with unexpectedly heavy resistance. I think the entire war is a fraud cooked up by the British as an excuse for seizing the canal. And we, we who have to execute this policy, even we were not told.

Pause.

Brock Well . . . what difference does it make?

Darwin My dear boy.

Brock I mean it.

Darwin Raymond.

Brock It makes no difference.

Darwin I was lied to.

Brock Yes, but you were against it from the start.

Darwin I . . .

Brock Oh come on, we all were. The Foreign Office hated the operation from the very first mention, so what difference does it make now?

Darwin All the difference in the world.

Brock None at all.

Darwin The government lied to me.

Brock If the policy was wrong, if it was wrong to begin with . . .

Darwin They are not in good faith.

Brock I see, I see, so what you're saying is, the British may do anything, doesn't matter how murderous, doesn't matter how silly, just so long as we do it in good faith.

Darwin Yes. I would have defended it, I wouldn't have minded how damn stupid it was. I would have defended it had it been honestly done. But this time we are cowboys and when the English are the cowboys, then in truth I fear for the future of the globe.

A pause. Darwin walks to the curtained window and stares out. Brock left sitting doesn't turn as he speaks.

Brock Prime Minister Eden is weak. For years he has been weak. For years people have taunted him, why aren't you strong? Like Churchill? He goes round, he begins to think, I must find somebody to be strong on. He finds Nasser. Now he'll show them. He does it to impress. He does it badly. No one is impressed.

Darwin turns to look at Brock.

Mostly what we do is what we think people expect of us. Mostly it's wrong. (*Pause.*) Are you going to resign?

The sound of laughter as Susan, Mme Aung, M. Aung and Alice stream into the room. Mme Aung is small, tidy and bright. Alice is spectacularly dressed.

Susan Mme Aung has been enthralling us with the story of the new Bergman film at the Everyman.

Darwin Ah.

Brock Ah yes.

Susan Apparently it's about depression, isn't that so, Mme Aung?

Mme. Aung I do feel the Norwegians are very good at that sort of thing.

Susan Is anything wrong? (*She stands and looks at Brock and Darwin.*) Please do sit down everyone. I'm sorry, I think we may have interrupted the men.

Brock It's all right.

Susan They were probably drafting a telegram . . .

Brock We weren't . . .

Susan That's what they do before they drop a bomb. They send their targets notice in a telegram. Bombs tonight, evacuate the area. Now what does that indicate to you, M. Aung?

Brock Susan, please.

Susan I'll tell you what it indicates to me. Bad conscience. They don't even have the guts to make a war any more.

Pause.

Darwin Perhaps Mme Aung will tell us the story of the film. This is something I'd be very keen to hear.

Mme Aung I feel the ladies have already . . .

Alice We don't mind.

Susan It's all right. Go ahead. We like the bit in the mental ward.

Mme Aung Ah yes.

Susan Raymond will like it. You got me out of the bin, didn't you, dear?

Brock Yes, yes.

Susan That's where he proposed to me. A moment of weakness. Of mine, I mean.

Brock Please, darling . . .

Susan I married him because he reminded me of my father.

Mme Aung Really?

Susan At that point, of course, I didn't realise just what a shit my father was.

Pause.

Alice I'm sorry. She has a sort of psychiatric cabaret.

Susan laughs.

Susan That's very good. And there's something about Suez which . . .

Brock Will you please be quiet? (*Pause.*) The story of the film.

Mme Aung is embarrassed. It takes her considerable effort to start.

Mme Aung There's a woman . . . who despises her husband . . .

Pause.

Susan Is it getting a little bit chilly in here? October nights. Those poor parachutists. I do know how they feel. Even now. Cities. Fields. Trees. Farms. Dark spaces. Lights. The parachute opens. We descend. (*Pause.*) Of course, we were comparatively welcome, not always ecstatic, not the Gaullists, of course, but by and large we did make it our business to land in countries where we were wanted. Certainly the men were. I mean, some of the relationships, I can't tell you. I remember a colleague telling me of the heat, of the smell of a particular young girl, the hot wet smell, he said. Nothing since. Nothing since then. I can't see the Egyptian girls somehow . . . no. Not in Egypt now. I mean, there were broken hearts when we left. I mean, there are girls today who mourn Englishmen who died in Dachau, died naked in Dachau, men with whom they had spent a single night. Well. (*Pause. The tears are pouring down her face, she can barely speak.*) But then . . . even for myself I do like to make a point of sleeping with men I don't know. I do find once you get to know them you usually don't want to sleep with them any more . . .

Brock gets up and shouts at the top of his voice across the room.

Brock Please can you stop, can you stop fucking talking for five fucking minutes on end?

Susan I would stop, I would stop, I would stop fucking talking if I ever heard anyone else say anything worth fucking stopping talking for.

Pause. Then Darwin moves.

Darwin I'm sorry. I apologise. I really must go. (*He crosses the room.*) M. Aung. Farewell.

Aung We are behind you, sir. There is wisdom in your expedition.

Darwin Thank you.

Aung May I say, sir, these gyps need whipping and you are the man to do it?

Darwin Thank you very much. Mme Aung.

Mme Aung We never really met.

Darwin No. No. We never met, that is true. But perhaps before I go, I may nevertheless set you right on a point of fact. Ingmar Bergman is not a bloody Norwegian, he is a bloody Swede. (*He nods slightly.*) Good night, everyone.

Darwin goes out. Brock gets up and goes to the door, then turns.

Brock He's going to resign.

Pause.

Susan Isn't this an exciting week? Don't you think? Isn't this thrilling? Don't you think? Everything is up for grabs. At last. We will see some changes. Thank the Lord. Now, there was dinner. I made some more dinner for Leonard. A little ham. And chicken. And some pickles and tomato. And lettuce. And there are a couple of pheasants in the fridge. And I can get twelve bottles of claret from the cellar. Why not? There is plenty. Shall we eat again?

Interval.

SCENE EIGHT

Knightsbridge. July 1961.

From the dark the voice of a Priest.

Priest Man that is born of woman hath but a short time to live and is full of misery. He cometh up and is cut down like a flower. He fleeth and never continueth in one stay. In the midst of life we are in death. Of whom may we seek for succour but of thee, O Lord, who for our sins art justly displeased?

The room is dark. All the chairs, all the furniture, all the mirrors are covered in white dust-sheets. There is a strong flood of light from the hall which silhouettes the group of three as they enter, all dressed in black. First Brock, then Dorcas, a tall, heavily built, seventeen-year-old blonde, and then Alice who, like the others, does not remove her coat. Alice's manner has darkened and sharpened somewhat. Brock goes to take the sheets off two chairs.

Brock I must say, I'd forgotten just how grim it can be.

Alice All that mumbling.

Brock I know. And those bloody hymns. They really do you no good at all. (*He wraps a sheet over his arm.*) Would you like to sit down in here? I'm afraid the whole house is horribly unused.

The women sit. Brock holds his hand out to Dorcas.

You and I haven't had a proper chance to meet.

Alice I hope you didn't mind . . .

Brock Not at all.

Alice . . . my bringing Dorcas along.

Brock She swelled the numbers.

Dorcas I had the afternoon off school.

Brock I'm not sure I'd have chosen a funeral . . .

Dorcas It was fine.

Brock Oh good.

Dorcas Alice told me that you were very good friends . . .

Brock Well, we are.

Dorcas . . . who she hadn't seen for a very long time and she was sure you wouldn't mind me . . . you know . . .

Brock Gatecrashing?

Dorcas Yes.

Brock At the grave.

Dorcas It sounds awful.

Brock You were welcome, as far as I was concerned.

Dorcas The only thing was . . . I never heard his name.

Brock His name was Darwin.

Dorcas Ah.

Susan stands unremarked in the doorway. She has taken her coat off and is plainly dressed in black, with some books under her arm. Her manner is quieter than before, and yet more elegant.

Susan Please, nobody get up for me.

She moves down to the front where there are two cases filled with books on the floor.

Brock Ah, Susan . . .

Susan I was just looking out some more books to take back.

Brock Are you all right?

Susan Yes, fine.

Alice Susan, this is Dorcas I told you about.

Susan How do you do?

Dorcas How do you do?

Susan tucks the books away.

Alice I teach Dorcas history.

Brock Good Lord, how long have you done that?

Alice Oh . . . I've been at it some time.

Dorcas Alice is a very good teacher, you know.

Brock I'm sure.

Alice Thank you, Dorcas.

Dorcas We had a poll and Alice came top.

They smile at each other. Unasked, Dorcas gives Alice a cigarette.

Alice Ta.

Brock Where do you teach?

Alice It's called the Kensington Academy.

Brock I see.

Alice It's in Shepherd's Bush.

Dorcas It's a crammer.

Alice For the daughters of the rich and the congenitally stupid. Dorcas to a T.

Dorcas It's true.

Alice There's almost nothing that a teacher can do.

Dorcas Alice says we're all the prisoners of our genes.

Alice When you actually try to engage their attention, you know that all they can really hear inside their heads is the great thump-thump of their ancestors fucking too freely among themselves.

Dorcas Nothing wrong with that.

Alice No?

Dorcas Stupid people are happier.

Alice Is that what you think?

They smile again. Brock watches.

Brock Well . . .

Susan Raymond, could you manage to make us some tea?

Brock Certainly, if there's time . . .

Susan I'm sure everyone's in need of it.

Brock smiles and goes out.

Alice rang me this morning. She said she was very keen we should meet.

Alice I didn't realise you were going back so soon.

Susan It's a problem, I'm afraid. My husband is a diplomat. We're posted in Iran. I haven't been to London for over three years. Then when I heard of Leonard's death I felt . . . I just felt very strongly I wanted to attend.

Dorcas Alice was saying he'd lost a lot of his friends.

Susan looks across at Alice.

Susan Yes, that's true.

Dorcas I didn't understand what . . .

Susan He spoke his mind over Suez. In public. He didn't hide his disgust. A lot of people never forgave him for that.

Dorcas Oh, I see. (*Pause.*) What's . . .

Alice It's a historical incident four years ago, caused a minor kind of stir at the time. It's also the name of a waterway in Egypt. Egypt is the big brown country up the top right-hand corner of Africa. Africa is a continent . . .

Dorcas Yes, thank you.

Alice And that's why nobody was there today.

Alice looks up at Susan but she has turned away.

I got that panic, you know, you get at funerals. I was thinking, I really don't want to think about death . . .

Susan Yes.

Alice Anything, count the bricks, count the trees, but don't think about death . . . (*She smiles.*) So I tried to imagine Leonard was still alive, I mean locked in his coffin but still alive. And I was laughing at how he would have dealt with the situation, I mean just exactly what the protocol would be.

Susan He would know it.

Alice Of course. Official procedure in the case of being buried alive. How many times one may tap on the lid. How to rise from the grave without drawing unnecessary attention to yourself.

Susan Poor Leonard.

Alice I know. But he did make me laugh.

Susan looks at her catching the old phrase. Then turns at once to Dorcas.

Susan Alice said I might help you in some way.

Dorcas Well, yes.

Susan Of course. If there's anything at all. (*She smiles.*)

Dorcas Did she tell you what the problem was?

Alice There isn't any problem. You need money, that's all.

Dorcas Alice said you'd once been a great friend of hers, part of her sort of crowd . . .

Susan Are they still going then?

Alice They certainly are.

Dorcas And that you might be sympathetic as you'd . . . well . . . as you'd known some troubles yourself . . .

Alice Dorcas needs cash from an impeccable source.

Pause.

Susan I see.

Dorcas I'd pay it back.

Susan Well, I'm sure.

Dorcas I mean it's only two hundred pounds. In theory I could still get it for myself, perhaps I'll have to, but Alice felt . . .

Alice Never mind.

Dorcas No, I think I should, I mean, I think I should say Alice did feel, as she'd introduced me to this man . . .

Pause. Alice looks away.

Just because he was one of her friends . . . which I just think is silly, I mean, for God's sake, I'm old enough to live my own life . . .

Susan Yes.

Dorcas I mean, I am seventeen. And I knew what I was doing. So why the hell should Alice feel responsible?

Susan I don't know.

Dorcas Anyway, the man was a doctor, one of Alice's famous bent doctors, you know, I just wanted to get hold of some drugs, but he wouldn't hand over unless I agreed to fool around, so I just . . . I didn't think anything of it . . .

Susan No.

Dorcas It just seemed like part of the price. At the time. Of course I never guessed it would be three months later and, wham, the knitting needles.

Susan Yes.

Pause.

Dorcas I mean, to be honest, I could still go to Daddy and tell him. Just absolutely outright tell him. Just say, Daddy, I'm sorry but . . .

Alice Wham, the knitting needles.

Dorcas Yes.

Susan looks across at Alice. The two women stare steadily at each other as Dorcas talks.

But of course one would need a great deal of guts. (*Pause.*) I mean, I can't tell you how awful I feel. I mean, coming straight from a funeral . . .

Susan suddenly gets up and walks to the door, speaking very quietly.

Susan Well, I'm sure it needn't delay us for too long . . .

Dorcas Do you mean . . .

Susan Kill a child. That's easy. No problem at all. (*She*

70

opens the door. She has heard Brock with the tea-tray outside.) Ah Raymond, the tea.

Brock I have to tell you the car has arrived.

Susan Oh good.

Brock The driver is saying we must get away at once.

Susan has gone out into the hall. Brock sets the tray down near Dorcas and Alice, and begins to pour.

It must be two years since I made my own tea. Persian labour is disgustingly cheap.

Dorcas I thought you said they . . .

Alice It's another name for Iran.

Dorcas Oh I see.

Susan has reappeared with her handbag and now goes to the writing desk. She folds the sheet back and lowers the lid.

Brock Susan, I do hope you're preparing to go.

Susan I will do, I just need a minute or two . . .

Brock I don't think we have time to do anything but . . .

Susan walks over to him.

Susan I do need some tea. Just to wash down my pill.

A pause. Brock smiles.

Brock Yes, of course.

Susan takes the cup from his hand. Then goes back to the desk where she gets out a cheque book and begins to write.

Alice So, Raymond, you must tell us about life in Iran.

Brock I would say we'd been very happy out there. Wouldn't you, Susan?

Susan Uh-huh.

Brock I think the peace has done us both a great deal of good. We were getting rather frenzied in our last few months here. (*He smiles.*)

Alice And the people?

Brock The people are fine. In so far as one's seen them, you know. It's only occasionally that you manage to get out. But the trips are startling, no doubt about that. There you are.

Brock hands Alice tea.

Alice Thank you.

Brock The sky. The desert. And of course the poverty. Living among people who have to struggle so hard. It can make you see life very differently.

Susan Do I make it to cash?

Alice If you could.

Brock hands Dorcas tea.

Dorcas Thanks.

Brock I do remember Leonard, that Leonard always said, the pleasure of diplomacy is perspective, you see. Looking across distances. For instance, we see England very clearly from there. And it does look just a trifle decadent.

He smiles again and drinks his tea.

Susan I'm lending Dorcas some money.

Brock Oh really, is that wise?

Alice She needs an operation.

Brock What?

Alice The tendons of her hands. If she's ever to play in a concert hall again.

Brock Do you actually play a . . .

Susan gets up from her desk.

Susan Raymond, could you take a look at that case? One of those locks is refusing to turn.

Brock Ah yes.

Brock goes to shut the case. Alice watches smiling as Susan walks across to Dorcas to hand her the cheque.

Susan Here you are.

Dorcas Thank you.

Susan Don't thank us. We're rotten with cash.

Brock closes the case. Susan gathers the cups on to the tray and places it by the door.

Brock If that's it, then I reckon we're ready to go. I'm sorry to turn you out of the house . . .

Alice That's all right.

Brock Alice, you must come and see us . . .

Alice I shall.

Brock My tour has been extended another two years. Dorcas, I'm happy to have met. I hope your studies proceed, under Alice's tutelage. In the meantime perhaps you might lend me a hand . . . (*He gestures at the case.*) Susan's lifeline. Her case full of books.

Dorcas goes to carry out the smaller case.

Susan, you're ready?

Susan Yes, I am.

Brock You'll follow me down?

Susan nods but doesn't move.

Well . . . I shall be waiting in the car.

Brock goes out with the large case. Dorcas follows.

Dorcas Alice, we won't be long, will we?

Alice No.

Dorcas It's just it's biology tonight and that's my favourite. (*Off.*) Do I put them in the boot?

Brock (*off*) If you could.

Susan and Alice left alone do not move.

Susan She's very stupid, isn't she?

Alice nods.

Alice But her body is superb.

A pause.

Susan I knew if I came over I would never return.

She pulls the sheet off the desk. It slinks on to the floor. Then she moves round the room, pulling away all the sheets from the furniture, letting them all fall. Then takes them from the mirrors. Then she lights the standard lamps, the table lamps. The room warms and brightens. Alice sits perfectly still, her legs outstretched. Then Susan turns to look at Alice.

You excite me.

Brock appears at the open door.

Brock Susan. Darling. Are we ready to go?

Whitehall. January 1962.

From the dark the sound of a radio interview. The Interviewer is male, serious, a little guarded.

Voice You were one of the few women to be flown into France?

Susan Yes.

Voice And one of the youngest?

Susan Yes.

Voice Did you always have complete confidence in the organisation that sent you?

Susan Yes, of course.

Voice Since the war it's frequently been alleged that Special Operations was amateurish, its recruitment methods were haphazard, some of its behaviour was rather cavalier. Did you feel that at the time?

Susan Not at all.

Voice The suggestion is that it was careless of human life. Did you feel that any of your colleagues died needlessly?

Susan I can't say.

Voice If you were to . . .

Susan Sorry, if I could . . .

Voice By all means.

Susan You believed in the organisation. You had to. If you didn't, you would die.

Voice But you must have had an opinion . . .

Susan No. I had no opinion. I have an opinion now.

Voice And that is?

Susan That it was one part of the war from which the British emerge with the greatest possible valour and distinction.

A slight pause.

Voice Do you ever get together with former colleagues and talk about the war?

Susan Never. We aren't clubbable.

The Foreign Office. A large room in Scott's Palazzo. A mighty painting above a large fireplace in an otherwise barish waiting room. It shows Britannia Colonorum Mater in pseudo-classical style. Otherwise the room is uncheering. A functional desk, some unremarkable wooden chairs, a green radiator. An air of functional disuse. Two people. Susan is standing at one side, smartly dressed again with coat and handbag; Begley stands opposite by an inner door. He is a thin young man with impeccable manners. He is twenty-two.

Begley Mrs Brock, Sir Andrew will see you now. He only has a few minutes, I'm afraid.

At once through the inner door comes Sir Andrew Charleson in a double-breasted blue suit. He is in his early fifties, dark-haired, thickening, almost indolent. He cuts less of a figure than Darwin but he has far more edge.

Charleson Ah, Mrs Brock.

Susan Sir Andrew.

Charleson How do you do?

Susan and Charleson shake hands.

We have met.

Susan That's right.

Charleson The Queen's Garden Party. And I've heard you on the wireless recently. Talking about the war. How extraordinary it must have been.

Pause.

Susan This must seem a very strange request.

Charleson Not in the slightest. We're delighted to see you here.

Begley takes two chairs out from the wall and places them down opposite each other.

Perhaps I might offer you a drink.

Susan If you are having one.

Charleson Unfortunately not. I'm somewhat liverish.

Susan I'm sorry.

Charleson No, no, it's a hazard of the job. Half the diplomats I know have bad offal, I'm afraid. (*He turns to Begley.*) If you could leave us, Begley.

Begley Sir.

Charleson Just shuffle some papers for a while.

Begley goes through the inner door. Charleson gestures Susan to sit.

You mustn't be nervous you know, Mrs Brock. I have to encounter many diplomatic wives, many even more distinguished than yourself, with very similar intent. It is much commoner than you suppose.

Susan Sir Andrew, as you know, I take very little part in my husband's professional life . . .

Charleson Indeed.

Susan Normally, I spend a great deal of time on my own . . . with one or two friends . . . of my own . . .

Mostly I like reading, I like reading alone . . . I do think to be merely your husband's wife is demeaning for a woman of any integrity at all . . .

Charleson smiles.

Charleson I understand.

Susan But I find for the first time in my husband's career I am beginning to feel some need to intervene.

Charleson I had a message, yes.

Susan I hope you appreciate my loyalty . . .

Charleson Oh yes.

Susan Coming here at all. Brock is a man who has seen me through some very difficult times . . .

Charleson I am told.

Susan But this is a matter on which I need to go behind his back.

Charleson gestures reassurance.

My impression is that since our recall from Iran he is in some way being penalised.

Charleson makes no reaction.

As I understand it, you're Head of Personnel . . .

Charleson I'm the Chief Clerk, yes . . .

Susan I've come to ask exactly what my husband's prospects are. (*Pause.*) I do understand the foreign service now. I know that my husband could never ask himself. Your business is conducted in a code, which it's considered unethical to break. Signs and indications are all you are given. Your stock is rising, your stock is falling . . .

Charleson Yes.

Susan Brock has been allocated to a fairly lowly job, backing up the EEC negotiating team . . .

Charleson He's part of the push into Europe, yes.

Susan The foreign posts he's since been offered have not been glittering.

Charleson We offered him Monrovia.

Susan Monrovia. Yes. He took that to be an insult. Was he wrong?

Charleson smiles.

Charleson Monrovia is not an insult.

Susan But?

Charleson Monrovia is more in the nature of a test. A test of nerve, it's true. If a man is stupid enough to accept Monrovia, then he probably deserves Monrovia. That is how we think.

Susan But you . . .

Charleson And Brock refused. (*He shrugs.*) Had we wanted to insult him there are far worse jobs. In this building too. In my view town-twinning is the *coup de grâce*. I'd far rather be a martyr to the tsetse fly than have to twin Rotherham with Bergen-op-Zoom.

Susan You are evading me.

Pause. Charleson smiles again.

Charleson I'm sorry. It's a habit, as you say. (*He pauses to rethink. Then with confidence:*) Your husband has never been a flyer, Mrs Brock.

Susan I see.

Charleson Everyone is streamed, a slow stream, a fast stream . . .

Susan My husband is slow?

Charleson Slowish.

Susan That means . . .

Charleson What is he? First Secretary struggling towards Counsellor. At forty-one it's not remarkable, you know.

Susan But it's got worse.

Charleson You think?

Susan The last six months. He's never felt excluded from his work before.

Charleson Does he feel that?

Susan I think you know he does.

Pause.

Charleson Well, I'm sure the intention was not to punish him. We have had some trouble in placing him, it's true. The rather startling decision to desert his post . . .

Susan That was not his fault.

Charleson We were told. We were sympathetic. Psychiatric reasons?

Susan I was daunted at the prospect of returning to Iran.

Charleson Of course. Persian psychiatry. I shudder at the thought. A heavy-handed people at the best of times. We understood. Family problems. Our sympathy goes out . . .

Susan But you are blocking his advance.

Charleson thinks, then changes tack again.

Charleson I think you should understand the basis of our talk. The basis on which I agreed to talk. You asked for information. The information is this: that Brock is making haste slowly. That is all I can say.

Susan I'm very keen he should not suffer on my account.

Susan's voice is low. Charleson looks at his hands.

Charleson Mrs Brock, believe me, I recognise your tone. Women have come in here and used it before.

Susan I would like to see my husband advance.

Charleson I also have read the stories in your file, so nothing in your manner is likely to amaze. I do know exactly the kind of person you are. When you have chosen a particular course . . . (*He pauses.*) When there is something which you very badly want . . . (*He pauses again.*) But in this matter I must tell you, Mrs Brock, it is more than likely you have met your match.

The two of them stare straight at each other.

We are talking of achievement at the highest level. Brock cannot expect to be cosseted through. It's not enough to be clever. Everyone here is clever, everyone is gifted, everyone is diligent. These are simply the minimum skills. Far more important is an attitude of mind. Along the corridor I boast a colleague who in 1945 drafted a memorandum to the government advising them not to accept the Volkswagen works as war reparation, because the Volkswagen plainly had no commercial future. I must tell you, unlikely as it may seem, that man has risen to the very, very top. All sorts of diplomatic virtues he displays. He has forbearance. He is gracious. He is sociable. Perhaps you begin to understand . . .

Susan You are saying . . .

Charleson I am saying that certain qualities are valued here above a simple gift of being right or wrong. Qualities sometimes hard to define . . .

Susan What you are saying is that nobody may speak, nobody may question . . .

Charleson Certainly tact is valued very high.

Pause. Susan, very low:

Susan Sir Andrew, do you never find it in yourself to despise a profession in which nobody may speak their mind?

Charleson That is the nature of the service, Mrs Brock. It is called diplomacy. And in its practice the English lead the world. (*He smiles.*) The irony is this: we had an empire to administer, there were six hundred of us in this place. Now it's to be dismantled and there are six thousand. As our power declines, the fight among us for access to that power becomes a little more urgent, a little uglier perhaps. As our influence wanes, as our empire collapses, there is little to believe in. Behaviour is all.

Pause.

This is a lesson which you both must learn.

A moment, then Susan picks up her handbag to go.

Susan I must thank you for your frankness, Sir Andrew . . .

Charleson Not at all.

Susan I must, however, warn you of my plan. If Brock is not promoted in the next six days, I am intending to shoot myself.

Susan gets up from her seat. Charleson follows quickly.

Now thank you, and I shan't stay for the drink . . .

Charleson (*calls*) Begley . . .

Susan I'm due at a reception for Australia Day.

Charleson moves quickly to the inner door. Susan begins talking very fast as she moves to go.

Charleson Begley.

Susan I always like to see just how rude I can be. Not that the Australians ever notice, of course. So it does become a sort of Zen sport, don't you think?

Begley appears.

Charleson John, I wonder, could you give me a hand?

Begley Sir.

Susan stops near the door, starts talking yet more rapidly.

Susan Ah, the side-kick, the placid young man, now where have I seen that character before?

Charleson If we could take Mrs Brock down to the surgery . . .

Susan I assure you, Sir Andrew, I'm perfectly all right.

Charleson Perhaps alert her husband . . .

Begley If you're not feeling well . . .

Susan People will be waiting at Australia House. I can't let them down. It will be packed with angry people all searching for me, saying where is she, what a let-down. I only came here to be insulted and now there's no chance.

Charleson looks at Begley as if to co-ordinate a move. They advance slightly.

Charleson I think it would be better if you . . .

Susan starts to shout.

Susan Please. Please leave me alone.

Charleson and Begley stop. Susan is hysterical. She waits a moment.

I can't . . . always manage with people. (*Pause.*) I think you have destroyed my husband, you see.

SCENE TEN

Knightsbridge. Easter 1962.

*From the dark the sound of some stately orchestral
chords: Mahler, melodic, solemn. It is evening. The room
has been restored to its former rather old-fashioned
splendour. The curtains are drawn. At a mahogany table
sits Alice. She is putting a large pile of leaflets into brown
envelopes. Very little disturbs the rhythm of her work.
She is dressed exactly as for Scene One.*

*Brock is sitting at another table at the front of the
stage. He has an abacus in front of him and a pile of
ledgers and cheque stubs. He is dressed in cavalry twills
with a check shirt open at the neck.*

The music stops. The stereo machine switches itself off.

Brock Well, I suppose it isn't too bad. Perhaps we'll keep
going another couple of years. A regime of mineral water
and lightly browned toast.

*He smiles and stretches. Then turns to look at Alice.
There is a bottle of mineral water on the table in front
of her.*

I assume she's still in there.

Alice She paces around.

Brock gets up and pours some out.

Brock I told her this morning . . . we'll have to sell the
house. I'm sure we can cope in a smaller sort of flat.
Especially now we don't have to entertain. (*He takes a
sip.*) I can't help feeling it will be better, I'm sure. Too
much money. I think that's what went wrong. Something
about it corrupts the will to live. Too many years spent
sploshing around. (*He suddenly listens.*) What?

Alice Nothing. She's just moving about.

Brock turns to Alice.

Brock Perhaps you'd enjoy to take the evening off. I'm happy to do duty for an hour or two.

Alice I enjoy it. I get to do my work. A good long slog for my charity appeal. And I've rather fallen out with all those people I knew. And most of them go off on the Ban the Bomb March.

Brock Really? Of course. Easter weekend. (*He picks his way through the remains of an Indian takeaway meal which is on Alice's table, searching for good scraps.*)

Alice Except for Alistair and I've no intention of spending an evening with him – or her, as he's taken to calling himself.

Brock How come?

Alice Apparently he's just had his penis removed.

Brock Voluntarily? It's what he intended, I mean?

Alice I believe. In Morocco. And replaced with a sort of pink plastic envelope. I haven't seen it. He says he keeps the shopping list in there, tucks five pound notes away, so he says.

Brock I thought that strange young girl of yours would ring.

Alice looks up for a moment from her work.

Alice No, no. She decided to move on. There's some appalling politician, I'm told. On the paedophiliac wing of the Tory party. She's going to spend the summer swabbing the deck on his yacht. Pleasuring his enormous underside. It's what she always wanted. The fat. The inane. (*She looks up again.*) If you've nothing to do, you could give a hand with these.

Brock takes no notice, casts aside the scraps.

Brock Looking back, I seem to have been eating all the time. My years in the Foreign Service, I mean. I don't think I missed a single canapé. Not one. The silver tray flashed and bang, I was there.

Alice Do you miss it?

Brock Almost all the time. There's not much glamour in insurance, you know. (*He smiles.*) Something in the Foreign Office suited my style. Whatever horrible things people say. At least they were hypocrites, I do value that now. Hypocrisy does keep things pleasant for at least part of the time. Whereas down in the City they don't even try.

Alice You chose it.

Brock That's right. That isn't so strange. The strange bit is always . . . why I remain. (*He stands staring a moment.*) Still, it gives her something new to despise. The sad thing is this time . . . I despise it as well.

Alice reaches for a typed list of names, pushes aside the pile of envelopes.

Alice Eight hundred addresses, eight hundred names . . .

Brock You were never attracted? A regular job?

Alice I never had time. Too busy relating to various young men. Falling in and out of love turns out to be like any other career. (*She looks up.*) I had an idea that lust . . . that lust was very good. And could be made simple. And cheering. And light. Perhaps I was simply out of my time.

Brock You speak as if it's over.

Alice I've no doubt it is.

Pause.

Brock How long since anyone took a look next door?

Alice That's why I think it may be time to do good.

Susan opens the door, standing dressed as for Scene One. She is a little dusty.

Susan I need to ask you to move out of here. I am in temporary need of this room. You can go wherever you like. And pretty soon also . . . you're welcome to return.

She goes off at once to the desk where she picks items off the surface and throws them quietly into cubbyholes. Alice is looking at Brock.

Brock You'd better tell me, Susan, what you've done to your hands.

Susan I've just been taking some paper from the wall.

Brock There's blood.

Susan A fingernail.

Pause.

Brock Susan, what have you actually done?

Brock gets up and goes to the door, looks down the corridor. Susan stands facing the desk, speaks quietly.

Susan I thought as we were going to get rid of the house . . . and I couldn't stand any of the things that were there . . .

Brock turns back into the room. She turns and looks at him.

Now what's best to be doing in here?

Brock looks at her, speaks as quietly.

Brock Could you look in the drawer please, Alice, there's some Nembutal . . .

Alice I'm not sure we should . . .

Brock I shan't ask you again.

Alice slides open the drawer, puts a small bottle of pills on the table. Brock moves a pace towards Susan.

Listen, if we're going to have to sell this house . . .

Susan You yourself said it, I've often heard you say, it's money that did it, it's money that rots. That we've all lived like camels off the fat in our humps. Well, then, isn't the best thing to do . . . to turn round simply and give the house away? (*She smiles.*) Alice, would this place suit your needs? Somewhere to set down all your unmarried mothers. If we lay out mattresses, mattresses on the floor . . .

Alice Well, I . . .

Susan Don't your women need a place to live? (*Without warning she raises her arms above her head.*) By our own hands.

Pause.

Of our own free will. An Iranian vase. A small wooden Buddha. Twelve marble birds copied from an Ottoman king.

Pause.

How can they be any possible use? Look out the bedroom window. I've thrown them away.

She opens the door and goes at once into the corridor. At once Brock crosses the room to the desk to look for his address book. Alice starts clearing up the leaflets and envelopes on the table in front of her.

Brock I suppose you conspired.

Alice Not at all.

Brock Well, really?

Alice That was the first that I've heard.

Brock In that case, please, you might give me some help. Find out what else she's been doing out there.

Susan reappears dragging in two packing cases, already half full. She then starts gathering objects from around the room.

Susan Cutlery, crockery, lampshades and books, books, books. Encyclopedias. Clutter. Meaningless. A universe of things. (*She starts to throw them one by one into the crates.*) Mosquito nets, golf clubs, photographs. China. Marble. Glass. Mementoes in stone. What is this shit? What are these God-forsaken bloody awful things?

Brock turns, still speaking quietly.

Brock Which is the braver? To live as I do? Or never, ever to face life like you? (*He holds up the small card he has found.*) This is the doctor's number, my dear. With my permission he can put you inside. I am quite capable of doing it tonight. So why don't you start to put all those things back?

A pause. Susan looks at him, then to Alice.

Susan Alice, would your women value my clothes?

Alice Well, I . . .

Susan It sounds fairly silly. I have thirteen evening dresses, though.

Brock Susan.

Susan Obviously not much use as they are. But possibly they could be recut. Resewn?

She reaches out and with one hand picks up an ornament from the mantelpiece which she throws with a crash into the crate. A pause.

Brock Your life is selfish, self-interested gain. That's the most charitable interpretation to hand. You claim to be protecting some personal ideal, always at a cost of almost infinite pain to everyone around you. You are selfish, brutish, unkind. Jealous of other people's happiness as well, determined to destroy other ways of happiness they find. I've spent fifteen years of my life trying to help you, simply trying to be kind, and my great comfort has been that I am waiting for some indication from you . . . some sign that you have valued this kindness of mine. Some love perhaps. Insane. (*He smiles.*) And yet . . . I really shan't ever give up, I won't surrender till you're well again. And that to me would mean your admitting one thing: that in the life you have led you have utterly failed, failed in the very, very heart of your life. Admit it. Then perhaps you might really move on. (*Pause.*) Now I'm going to go and give our doctor a ring. I plan at last to beat you at your own kind of game. I am going to play as dirtily and ruthlessly as you. And this time I am certainly not giving in.

He goes out. A pause.

Susan Well. (*Pause.*) Well, goodness. What's best to do? (*Pause.*) What's the best way to start stripping this room?

Susan doesn't move. Alice stands watching.

Alice Susan, I think you should get out of this house.

Susan Of course.

Alice I'll help you. Any way I can.

Susan Well, that's very kind.

Alice If you . . .

Susan I'll be going just as soon as this job is done.

Pause.

Alice Listen, if Raymond really means what he says . . .

Susan turns and looks straight at Alice.

You haven't even asked me, Susan, you see. You haven't asked me yet what I think of the idea.

Susan frowns.

Susan Really, Alice, I shouldn't need to ask. It's a very sad day when one can't help the poor . . .

Alice suddenly starts to laugh. Susan sets off across the room, resuming a completely normal social manner.

Alice For God's sake, Susan, he'll put you in the bin.

Susan Don't be silly, Alice, it's Easter weekend. It must have occurred to you . . . the doctor's away.

Brock reappears at the open door, the address book in his hand. Susan turns to him.

All right, Raymond? Anything I can do? I've managed to rout out some whisky over here. (*She sets the bottle down on the table, next to the Nembutal.*) Alice was just saying she might slip out for a while. Give us a chance to sort our problems out. I'm sure if we had a really serious talk . . . I could keep going till morning. Couldn't you? (*She turns to Alice.*) All right, Alice?

Alice Yes. Yes, of course. I'm going, I'm just on my way. (*She picks up her coat and heads for the door.*) All right if I get back in an hour or two? I don't like to feel I'm intruding. You know?

She smiles at Susan. Then closes the door. Susan at once goes back to the table. Brock stands watching her.

Susan Now, Raymond. Good. Let's look at this thing.

She pours out a spectacularly large Scotch, filling the glass to the very rim. Then she pushes it a few inches across the table to Brock.

Where would be the best place to begin?

SCENE ELEVEN

Blackpool. June 1962.

From the dark music. Then silence. Two voices in the dark.

Lazar Susan. Susan. Feel who I am.

Susan I know. I know who you are. How could you be anyone else but Lazar?

And a small bedside light comes on. Lazar and Susan are lying sideways across a double bed, facing opposite ways. They are in a sparsely furnished and decaying room. Lazar is in his coat, facing away from us as he reaches for the nightlight. Susan is also fully dressed, in a big black man's overcoat, her hair wild, her dress crumpled round her thighs. The bedside light barely illuminates them at all.

Jesus. Jesus. To be happy again.

At once Susan gets up and goes into what must be the bathroom. A shaft of yellow light from the doorway falls across the bed.

Lazar Don't take your clothes off whatever you do.

Susan *(off)* Of course not.

Lazar That would spoil it hopelessly for me.

Susan *(off)* I'm getting my cigarettes. I roll my own . . .

Lazar Goodness me.

Susan Tell you, there are no fucking flies on me.

She has reappeared with her holdall which is crumpled an stained. She sits cross-legged on the end of the bed. She starts to roll two cigarettes.

Lazar I am glad I found you.

Susan I'm just glad I came.

Lazar This place is filthy.

Susan It's a cheap hotel.

Lazar They seem to serve you dust on almost everything.

Susan You should be grateful for dust, did you know? If it weren't for all the dust in the atmosphere, human beings would be killed by the heat of the sun.

Lazar In Blackpool?

Susan Well . . .

Lazar Are you kidding me?

Susan reaches into the overcoat pocket.

Susan I was given some grass. Shall I roll it in?

Lazar Just the simple cigarette for me.

Susan nods.

I hope you didn't mind my choosing Blackpool at all. It's just that I work near . . .

Susan Don't tell me any more.

Lazar Susan . . . (*Pause.*) Will you . . . can you touch me again?

Susan facing away doesn't move, just smiles. A pause.

Do you know how I found you? Through the BBC. I just caught that programme a few months ago. They told me you were married and based in London now. They gave me an address . . .

Susan I left it weeks ago.

Lazar I know. I gather you've been out on the road.

But . . . I went, I went round and saw the man.

Susan And how was he?

Lazar He looked like a man who'd spent his life with you.

Susan How can you say that?

Lazar (*smiles*) Oh I'm guessing, that's all.

Susan smiles again.

He said he'd only just managed to reclaim.

Susan Oh really? That's my fault. I gave the house away.

Lazar He said he'd had to fight to get back into his home. There'd been some kind of trouble. Police, violence it seems . . .

Susan Was he angry?

Lazar Angry? No. He just seemed very sorry not to be with you.

Pause. Susan stops rolling the cigarette.

Susan Listen. I have to tell you I've not always been well. I have a weakness. I like to lose control. I've been letting it happen, well, a number of times . . .

Lazar Is it . . . ?

Susan I did shoot someone about ten years ago.

Lazar Did you hurt him?

Susan Fortunately no. At least that's what we kept telling him, you know. Raymond went and gave him money in notes. He slapped them like hot poultices all over his wounds. I think it did finally convince him on the whole. It was after Raymond's kindness I felt I had to get engaged . . .

Lazar Why do people . . .

Susan Marry? I don't know. Are you . . .

Pause.

Lazar What? Ask me anything at all.

Susan No. It's nothing. I don't want to know. (*She smiles again.*)

Lazar Do you ever see him?

Susan Good gracious no. I've stripped away everything, everything I've known. There's only one kind of dignity, that's in living alone. The clothes you stand up in, the world you can see . . .

Lazar Oh Susan . . .

Susan Don't. (*Pause. She is suddenly still.*) I have to believe that there's someone, you see. Somebody else who's been living like me.

Lazar looks across at Susan's back.

Lazar Can you remember?

Susan I remember it all. I remember it clearly as if it were today.

Lazar Did you think . . .

Susan I thought nothing at all. I felt. I simply let myself feel . . .

Lazar I remember the pines. And how larches smell. And thinking, my God, I do love this girl.

Susan You knew me two hours.

Lazar And I do love this girl.

Pause. Susan does not turn round. Lazar suddenly gets up, and goes to get his coat and gloves from his suitcase. Susan looks down at the unmade cigarette in her hands. Then she starts to make the roll-up again.

95

Susan How long till dawn? Do you think we should go? If we wait till morning we'll have to pay the bill. I can't believe that can be the right thing to do. (*She smiles.*) Is there an early train, do you know? Though just where I'm going I'm not really sure. There aren't many people who'll have me, you know . . . (*Pause.*) I hope you'll forgive me. The grass has gone in.

She licks along the edge of the joint, then lights it.
Lazar stands still, his suitcase beside him.

Lazar I don't know what I'd expected.

Susan Mmm?

Lazar What I'd hoped for, at the time I returned. Some sort of edge to the life that I lead. Some sort of feeling their death was worthwhile. (*Pause.*) Some day I must tell you. I don't feel I've done well. I gave in. Always. All along the line. Suburb. Wife. Hell. I work in a corporate bureaucracy as well . . .

Susan has begun to giggle.

Susan Lazar, I'm sorry. I'm just about to go.

Lazar What?

Susan I've eaten nothing. So I just go . . . (*She waves vaguely with her hand. Then smiles. A pause.*)

Lazar I hate, I hate this life that we lead.

Susan Oh, God, here I go. (*Pause.*) Kiss me. Kiss me now as I go.

Lazar moves towards Susan and tries to take her in his arms. But as he tries to kiss her, she falls back on to the bed, flopping down where she stays.
Lazar removes the roach from her hand. Puts it out. Goes over and closes his case. Then picks it up. Goes to the bathroom and turns the light off. Now only the nightlight is on. Lazar goes to the door.

Lazar A fine undercover agent will move so that nobody can ever tell he was there.

He turns the nightlight off. Darkness.

Susan Tell me your name.

Pause.

Lazar Codename. (*Pause.*) Codename. (*Pause.*) Codename Lazar.

Lazar opens the door of the room. At once music plays. Where you would expect a corridor you see the fields of France shining brilliantly in a fierce green square. The room scatters.

SCENE TWELVE

St Benoît, August 1944.
The darkened areas of the room disappear and we see a French hillside in high summer. The stage picture forms piece by piece. Green, yellow, brown. Trees. The fields stretch away. A high sun. A brilliant August day. Another Frenchman stands looking down into the valley. He carries a spade, is in wellingtons and corduroys. He is about forty, fattish with an unnaturally gloomy air.
Then Susan appears climbing the hill. She is nineteen. She is dressed like a young French girl, her pullover over her shoulder. She looks radiantly well.

Frenchman Bonjour, ma'moiselle.

Susan Bonjour.

Frenchman Vous regardez le village?

Susan Oui, je suis montée la colline pour mieux voir. C'est merveilleux.

Frenchman Oui. Indeed the day is fine.

Pause. Susan looks across at the Frenchman.

We understand. We know. The war is over now.

Susan 'I climbed the hill to get a better view.' (*She smiles.*) I've only spoken French for months on end.

Frenchman You are English?

Susan nods.

Tower Bridge.

Susan Just so.

The Frenchman smiles and walks over to join Susan. Together they look away down the hill.

Frenchman You join the party in the village?

Susan Soon. I'm hoping, yes, I'm very keen to go.

Frenchman Myself I work. A farmer. Like any other day. The Frenchman works or starves. He is the piss. The shit. The lowest of the low.

Susan moves forward a little, staring down the hill.

Susan Look. They're lighting fires in the square. And children . . . coming out with burning sticks. (*Pause.*) Have you seen anything as beautiful as this?

Susan stands looking out. The Frenchman mumbles ill-humouredly.

Frenchman The harvest is not good again this year.

Susan I'm sorry.

The Frenchman shrugs.

Frenchman As I expect. The land is very poor. I have to work each moment of the day.

Susan But you'll be glad, I think. You're glad as well?

Susan turns, so the Frenchman cannot avoid the question. He reluctantly concedes.

Frenchman I'm glad. Is something good, is true. (*He looks puzzled.*) The English . . . have no feelings, yes? Are stiff.

Susan They hide them, hide them from the world.

Frenchman Is stupid.

Susan Stupid, yes. It may be . . .

Pause.

Frenchman Huh?

Susan That things will quickly change. We have grown up. We will improve our world.

The Frenchman stares at Susan. Then offers gravely:

Frenchman Perhaps . . . perhaps you like some soup. My wife.

Susan All right.

Susan smiles. They look at each other, about to go.

Frenchman The walk is down the hill. Comrade.

Susan My friend. (*Pause.*) There will be days and days and days like this.

End.